Praise for *The Imaginary Girlfriend*

"The nearest thing to an autobiography Irving has written . . . Worth saving and savoring."

—*Seattle Times*

"*The Imaginary Girlfriend* is a miniature autobiography detailing Irving's parallel careers of writing and wrestling. . . . Tales of encounters with writers (John Cheever, Nelson Algren, Kurt Vonnegut) are intertwined with those about his wrestling teammates and coaches. With humor and compassion, [Irving] details the few truly important lessons he learned about writing. . . . And in beefing up his narrative with anecdotes that are every bit as hilarious as the antics in his novels, Irving combines the lessons of both obsessions (wrestling and writing) . . . into a somber reflection on the importance of living well."

—*Denver Post*

"*The Imaginary Girlfriend* . . . should be required reading for anyone who wants to write."

—Susan Cheever

"Irving's wrestling coaches, his writing mentors, and his family are vivid, inviting readers into a colorful world."

—*USA Today*

"A masterpiece . . . The generosity of spirit that marks his fiction leaks into his memoir in tender and surprising ways."

—*Edmonton Journal*

"What's best about this memoir is that Irving, fine storyteller that he is, somehow sidesteps the limelight. What this piece is really about is mentorship and friendship and the feelings Irving carries for those who have helped him make his way. It is but another display of the wide and generous spirit that powers the best of Irving's fiction."

—*BookPage*

THE
IMAGINARY
GIRLFRIEND

THE IMAGINARY GIRLFRIEND

A Memoir

JOHN IRVING

ARCADE PUBLISHING · NEW YORK

First Arcade/Skyhorse Paperback Edition 2022

Arcade Publishing books may be purchased in bulk at special discounts for sales promotion, corporate gifts, fund-raising, or educational purposes. Special editions can also be created to specifications. For details, contact the Special Sales Department, Arcade Publishing, 307 West 36th Street, 11th Floor, New York, NY 10018 or arcade@skyhorsepublishing.com.

Arcade Publishing® is a registered trademark of Skyhorse Publishing, Inc.®, a Delaware corporation.

Visit our website at www.arcadepub.com.
Visit the author's website at www.john-irving.com.

10 9 8 7 6 5 4 3 2 1

Library of Congress Cataloging-in-Publication Data is available on file.

Cover design by Brian Peterson
Cover photograph: '61 PEAN

Print ISBN: 978-1-956763-15-7
Ebook ISBN: 978-1-62872-412-7

Printed in the United States of America

CONTENTS

ACKNOWLEDGMENTS

A portion of "The Imaginary Girlfriend" first appeared in a fall 1995 issue of *The New Yorker*.

THE
IMAGINARY
GIRLFRIEND

Faculty Brat

In my prep-school days, at Exeter, Creative Writing wasn't taught—the essay was all-important there—but in my years at the academy I nevertheless wrote more short stories than anything else; I showed them (out of class) to George Bennett, my best friend's father. The late Mr. Bennett was then Chairman of the English Department; he was my first critic and encourager—I needed his help. Because I failed both Latin and math, I was required to remain at the academy for an unprecedented fifth year; yet I qualified for a course called English 4W—the "W" stood for Writing of the kind I wanted to do—and in this selective gathering I was urged to be Creative, which I rarely managed to be.

In my memory, which is subject to doubt, the star author and most outspoken critic in English 4W was my wrestling teammate Chuck Krulak, who was also known as "Brute" and who would become General Charles C. Krulak—the Commandant of the Marine Corps and a member of the Joint Chiefs of Staff. No less a presence, and as sarcastic a critic as the future General Krulak, was my classmate in English 5, the future writer G. W. S. Trow; he was just plain George then, but he was as sharp as a ferret—I feared his bite. It was only recently, when I was speaking with George, that he surprised me by saying he'd been deeply unhappy at Exeter; George had always struck me as being too confident to be unhappy—whereas my own state of mind at the time was one of perpetual embarrassment.

I could never have qualified for Exeter through normal admissions procedures; I was a weak student—as it turned out, I was dyslexic, but no one knew this at the time. Nevertheless, I was automatically admitted to the academy in the category of faculty child. My father taught in the History Department; he'd majored in Slavic Languages and Literature at Harvard—he was the first to teach Russian History at Exeter. I initiated a heightened level of intrafamily awkwardness by enrolling in his Russian History course. Dad rewarded me with a C+.

To say that Exeter was hard for me is an understatement. I was the only student in my Genetics class who failed to control his fruit-fly experiment. The red eyes and the white eyes were interbreeding so rapidly that I lost track of the generations; I attempted to dispose of the evidence in the drinking fountain outside the lab—not knowing that fruit flies could live (and breed) for days in the water pipes. When the unusable drinking fountain was declared "contaminated"—it was literally crawling with wet fruit flies—I crawled forth and made my confession.

I was forgiven by Mr. Mayo-Smith, the biologist who taught Genetics, because I was the only townie (a resident of Exeter) in any of his classes who owned a gun; the biologist needed me—more specifically, he needed my gun. Boarding students, quite understandably, were not allowed firearms. But as a New Hampshire native—"Live Free or Die," as the license plates say—I had an arsenal of weapons at my disposal; the biologist used me as the marksman who provided his Introductory Biology class with pigeons. I used to shoot them off the roof of the biologist's barn. Fortunately, Mr. Mayo-Smith lived some distance from town.

Yet even in my capacity as Mr. Mayo-Smith's marksman, I was a failure. He wanted the pigeons killed immediately after they'd eaten; that way the students who dissected them could examine the food contained in their crops. And so I allowed the pigeons to feed in the biologist's cornfield. When I flushed them from the field, they were so stupid: they always flew to the roof of his barn. It was a slate roof; when I picked them off—I used a 4X scope and a .22 long-rifle bullet, being careful not to shoot them in their crops—they slid down one side of the roof or the other. One day, I shot a hole in the roof; after that, Mr. Mayo-Smith never let me forget how his barn leaked. The fruit flies in the drinking fountain were the school's problem, but I had shot the biologist's very own barn—"Personal property, and all that that entails," as my father was fond of saying in Russian History.

Shooting a hole in Mr. Mayo-Smith's barn was less humiliating than the years I spent in Language Therapy. At Exeter, poor spelling was unknown—I mean that little was known about it. It was my dyslexia, of course, but—because that diagnosis wasn't available in the late 1950s and early '60s—bad spelling like mine was considered a psychological problem by the language therapist who evaluated my mysterious case. (The handicap of a language disability did not make my struggles at the academy any easier.)

When the repeated courses of Language Therapy were judged to have had no discernible influence on my ability to recognize the difference between "allegory" and "allergy," I was turned over to the school psychiatrist.

Did I hate the school?

"No." (I had grown up at the school!)

Why did I refer to my stepfather as my "father"?

"Because I love him and he's the only 'father' I've ever known."

But why was I "defensive" on the subject of other people calling my father my stepfather?

"Because I love him and he's the only 'father' I've ever known— why shouldn't I be 'defensive'?"

Why was I angry?

"Because I can't spell."

But why *couldn't* I spell?

"Search me."

Was it "difficult" having my stepfather—that is, my father—as a teacher?

"I had my father as a teacher for one year. I've been at the school, and a bad speller, for five years."

But why was I angry?

"Because I can't spell—and I have to see *you*."

"We certainly *are* angry, aren't we?" the psychiatrist said.

"I certainly *are*," I said. (I was trying to bring the conversation back to the subject of my *language* disability.)

* * *

An Underdog

There was one place at Exeter where I was never angry; I never lost my temper in the wrestling room—possibly because I wasn't embarrassed to be there. It is surprising that I felt so comfortable with wrestling. My athletic skills had never been significant. I had loathed Little League baseball. (By association, I hate all sports with balls.) I more mildly disliked skiing and skating. (I have a limited tolerance for cold weather.) I did have an inexplicable taste for physical contact, for the adrenal stimulation of bumping into people, but I was too small to play football; also, there was a ball involved.

When you love something, you have the capacity to bore everyone about *why*—it doesn't matter why. Wrestling, like boxing, is a weight-class sport; you get to bump into people your own size. You can bump into them very hard, but where you land is reasonably soft. And there are civilized aspects to the sport's combativeness: I've always admired the rule that holds you responsible, *if* you lift your opponent off the mat, for your opponent's "safe return." But the best answer to why I love wrestling is that it was the first thing I was any good at. And what limited success I had in the sport I owe completely to my first coach, Ted Seabrooke.

Coach Seabrooke had been a Big 10 Champion and a two-time All-American at Illinois; he was *way* overqualified for the job of coaching wrestling at Exeter—his teams dominated New England prep-school and high-school wrestling for years. An NCAA runner-up at 155 pounds, Ted Seabrooke was a handsome man; he weighed upward of 200 pounds in my time at the academy. He would sit on the mat with his legs spread in front of him; his arms were bent at the elbow but reaching out to you from the level of his chest. Even in such a vulnerable position, he could completely defend himself; I never saw anyone manage to get behind him. On his rump, he could scuttle like a crab—his feet tripping you, his legs scissoring you, his hands tying up your hands or snapping your head down. He could control you by holding you in his lap (a crab ride) or by taking possession of your near leg and your far arm (a cross-body ride); he was always gentle with you, and never seemed to expend much energy in the process of frustrating you. (Coach Seabrooke would first get diabetes and then die of cancer. At his memorial service, I couldn't speak half the eulogy I'd written for him, because I knew by heart the parts that would make me cry if I tried to say them aloud.)

Not only did Ted Seabrooke teach me how to wrestle; more important, he forewarned me that I would never be better than "halfway decent" as a wrestler—because of my limitations as an athlete. He also impressed upon me how I could compensate for my shortcomings: I had to be especially dedicated—a thorough student of the sport—if I wished to overcome my lack of any observable ability. "Talent is overrated," Ted told me. "That you're not very talented needn't be the end of it."

A high-school wrestling match is six minutes long, divided into three two-minute periods—with no rest between the periods. In the first period, both wrestlers start on their feet—a neutral position, with neither wrestler having an advantage. In the second period, in those days, one wrestler had the choice of taking the top or the bottom position; in the third period, the choice of positions was reversed. (Nowadays, the options of choice have been expanded to include the neutral position, and the wrestler given the choice in the second period may defer his choice until the third.)

What Coach Seabrooke taught me was that I should keep the score close through two periods—close enough so that one takedown or a reversal in the third period could win the match. And I needed to avoid "mix-ups"—free-for-all situations that were not in either wrestler's control. (The outcome of such a scramble favors the better athlete.) Controlling the pace of the match—a combination of technique, correct position, and physical conditioning—was my objective. I know it sounds boring—I was a boring wrestler. The pace that worked for me was slow. I liked a low-scoring match.

I rarely won by a fall; in five years of wrestling at Exeter, I probably pinned no more than a half-dozen opponents. I was almost never pinned—only twice, in fact.

I won 5–2 when I dominated an opponent; I won 2–1 or 3–2 when I was lucky, and lost 3–2 or 4–3 when I was less lucky. If I got the first takedown, I could usually win; if I lost the first takedown, I was hard-pressed to recover—I was not a come-from-behind man. I was, as Coach Seabrooke said, "halfway decent" as a counter-wrestler, too. But if my opponent was a superior athlete, I couldn't afford to rely on my counter-moves to his first shots; my counters weren't quick enough—my *reflexes* weren't quick enough. Against a superior athlete, I would take the first shot; against a superior *wrestler*, I would try to counter his first move.

"Or vice versa, if it's not working," Coach Seabrooke used to say. He had a sense of humor. "Where the head goes, the body must follow—usually," Ted would add. And: "An underdog is in a position to take a healthy bite."

This was a concept of myself that I'd been lacking. I was an underdog; therefore, I had to control the pace—of *everything*. This was more than I learned in English 4W, but the concept was applicable to my Creative Writing—and to all my schoolwork, too. If my classmates could read our history assignment in an hour, I allowed myself two or three. If I couldn't learn to spell, I would keep a list of my most frequently misspelled words—and I kept the list with me; I had it handy even for unannounced quizzes. Most of all, I rewrote everything; first drafts were like the first time you tried a new takedown—you needed to drill it, over and over again, before you even dreamed of trying it in a match. I began to take my lack of talent seriously.

An imperious Spanish teacher was fond of abusing those of us who lacked perfection with the insensitive (not to mention elitist) remark that we would all end up at Wichita State. I didn't know that Wichita was in Kansas; I knew only that this was a slur—if we weren't *talented* enough for Harvard, then Wichita State would be our just reward. Fuck you, I thought: my objective would then be to do well at Wichita State. Ted Seabrooke had gone to Illinois. I didn't suppose that this Spanish teacher thought too highly of Illinois either.

I remember telling Ted that I'd had two likable Spanish teachers, and one unlikable one. "I wouldn't complain about those odds," he said.

The Half-Pound Piece of Toast

My time at the academy was marked by two important transitions in Exeter wrestling under Coach Seabrooke. First, the wrestling room was moved from the basement of the old gymnasium to the upper reaches of the indoor track, which was called "the cage." The new room, high in the rafters, was exceedingly warm; from the hard-packed dirt of the track below us, and from the wooden track that circumscribed the upper level, came the steady pounding of the runners. Once our wrestling practice was underway, we wrestlers never heard the runners. The wrestling room was closed off from the wooden track by a heavy sliding door. Before and after practice, the door was open; during practice, the door was closed.

The other wrestling-related change that marked my time at Exeter was the mats themselves. I began wrestling on horsehair mats, which were covered with a filmy, flexible plastic; as a preventive measure against mat burns, this plastic sheeting was modestly effective, but—like the sheet on a bed—it loosened with activity. The loose folds were a cause of ankle injuries; also, the shock-absorbing abilities of those old horsehair mats were nonexistent in comparison to the comfort of the *new* mats that arrived at Exeter in time to be installed in the new wrestling room.

The new mats were smooth on the surface, with no cover. When the mats were warm, you could drop an egg from knee height and the egg wouldn't break. (Whenever someone tried this and the egg broke, we said that the mat wasn't warm enough.) On a cold gym floor, the texture of the mat would radically change. Later, I kept a wrestling mat in my unheated Vermont barn; in midwinter the mat was as hard as a floor.

Most of our dual-meet matches were also held in the cage, but not in the wrestling room where we practiced. An L-shaped wooden parapet extended like an arm off the wooden track. From this advantage—and from a loop of the wooden track itself—as many as 200 or 300 spectators could look down upon a less-than-regulation-size basketball court, where we rolled out the mats. There was barely enough floor space left over for a dozen or more rows of bleacher seats; most of our fans were above us, on the wooden track and parapet. It was like wrestling at the bottom of a teacup; the surrounding crowd peered over the rim of the cup.

Where we wrestled was appropriately called "the pit." The smell of dirt from the nearby track was strangely remindful of summer, although wrestling is a winter sport. What with the constant opening of the outside door, the pit was never a warm place; the mats, which were so warm and soft in the wrestling room, were cold and hard for the competition. And, when our wrestling meets coincided with track meets in the cage, the sound of the starting gun reverberated in the pit. I always wondered what the visiting wrestlers thought of the gunfire.

My first match in the pit was a learning experience. First-year wrestlers, or even second-year wrestlers, are not often starters on prep-school or high-school wrestling teams of any competitive quality. In New Hampshire, in the 1950s, wrestling—unlike baseball or basketball or hockey or skiing—was not something every kid grew up doing. There are certain illogical things to learn about any sport; wrestling, especially, does not come naturally. A double-leg takedown is _not_ like a head-on tackle in football. Wrestling is not about knocking a man down—it's about controlling him. To take a man down by his legs, you have to do more than knock his legs out from under him: you have to get your hips under your opponent, so that you can lift him off the mat before you put him down—this is only one example. Suffice it to say that a first-year wrestler is at a considerable disadvantage when wrestling anyone with experience—regardless of how physically strong or well-conditioned the first-year wrestler is.

I forget the exact combination of illness or injury or deaths-in-a-family (or all three) that led to my first match in the pit; as a first-year wrestler, I was quite content to practice wrestling with other first-year or second-year wrestlers. There was a "ladder" posted in the wrestling room, by weight class; in my first year, I would have been as low as fourth or fifth on the ladder at 133 pounds. But the varsity man was sick or hurt, and the junior-varsity man failed to make weight—and possibly the boy who was next-in-line had gone home for the weekend because his parents were divorcing. Who knows? For whatever reason, I was the best available body in the 133-pound class.

I was informed of this unwelcome news in the dining hall where I worked as a waiter at a faculty table; fortunately, I had not yet eaten my breakfast—I would have had to vomit it up. As it was, I was four pounds over the weight class and I ran for almost an hour on the wooden track of the indoor cage; I ran in a ski parka and other winter clothing. Then I skipped rope in the wrestling room for half an hour, wearing a rubber suit with a hooded sweat-shirt over it. I was an eighth of a pound under 133 at the weigh-ins, where I had my first look at my opponent—Vincent Buonomano, a defending New England Champion from Mount Pleasant High School in Providence, Rhode Island.

Had we forfeited the weight class, we could not have done worse: a forfeit counts the same as a pin—six points. It was Coach Seabrooke's hope that I wouldn't be pinned. In those days, a loss by decision was only a three-point loss for the team, regardless of how lopsided the score of the individual match. My goal, in other words, was to take a beating and lose the team only three points instead of six.

For the first 15 or 20 seconds, this goal seemed feasible; then I was taken down, to my back, and I spent the remainder of the period in a neck bridge—I had a strong neck. The choice was mine in the second period: on Coach Seabrooke's advice, I chose the top position. (Ted knew that I was barely surviving on the bottom.) But Buonomano reversed me immediately, and so I spent the better part of the second period fighting off my back, too. My only points were for escapes—unearned, because Buonomano let me go; he was guessing it might be easier to pin me directly following a takedown. One such takedown dropped me on my nose—both my hands were trapped, so that I couldn't break my fall. (It's true what they say about "seeing stars.")

When they stop a wrestling match to stop bleeding, there's no clock counting the injury time; this is because you can't fake bleeding. For other injuries, a wrestler is allowed no more than 90 seconds of injury time—accumulated in the course of the match. In this case, they weren't timing my nose bleed; when the trainer finished stuffing enough cotton up my nostrils to stanch the flow of blood, my dizziness had abated and I looked at the time remaining on the match clock—only 15 seconds! I had every confidence that I could stay off my back for another 15 seconds, and I told Ted Seabrooke so.

"It's only the second period," Seabrooke said.

I survived the 15 seconds but was pinned about midway into the third period—"With less than a minute to go," my mother lamentably told me.

The worst thing about being pinned in the pit was the lasting image of all those faces peering down at you. When you were winning, the fans were loud; when you were on your back, they were quiet, and their expressions were strangely incurious—as if they were already distancing themselves from your defeat.

I was never pinned in the pit again; the only other loss I remember there was by injury default—I broke my hand. When the trainer offered me the slop bucket—I needed to spit—I saw the orange rinds and a bloody towel in the bottom of the bucket, and I promptly fainted. Aside from that misfortune, and my first-ever match—with Mount Pleasant's Vincent Buonomano—I associated the pit with winning; my best matches were there. It was in the pit that I wrestled New England Champion Anthony Pieranunzi of East Providence High School to a 1–1 draw. I was not so lucky with Pieranunzi in the New England Championship tournament, where he beat me two years in a row; despite two undefeated dual-meet seasons, I never won a New England title.

My years at Exeter were the final years when the winner of the New England tournament won a truly *All*-New England title; 1961 was the last year that high schools and prep schools competed together in a year-end tournament—I was captain of the Exeter team that year. After that, there were separate private-school and public-school tournaments—a pity, I think, since high-school and prep-school wrestlers have much to learn from each other. But, by '61, the New England Interscholastic tournament, as it used to be called, had already grown too large.

I remember my last bus ride with the Exeter team, to East Providence—to the home mats of my nemesis, Anthony Pieranunzi. We'd checked our weight on the scales in the academy gym at about 5:00 in the morning; we were all under our respective weight classes—in some cases, barely. The bus left Exeter in darkness, which near Boston gave way to a dense winter fog; the snow, the sky, the trees, the road—all were shades of gray.

Our 121-pounder, Larry Palmer, was worried about his weight. He'd been only a quarter of a pound under at Exeter—the official weigh-ins were at East Providence. What if the scales were different? (They weren't supposed to be.) I'd been a half-pound under my 133-pound class; my mouth was dry, but I didn't dare drink any water—I was spitting in a paper cup. Larry was spitting in a cup, too. "Just don't eat," Coach Seabrooke told us. "Don't eat and don't drink—you're not going to gain weight on the bus."

Somewhere south of Boston, we stopped at a Howard Johnson's; this is what Larry Palmer remembers—I don't remember the Howard Johnson's because I didn't get off the bus. A few of our wrestlers were safely enough under their weight classes so that they could risk eating something; most of them at least got off the bus—to pee. I'd had nothing to eat or drink for about 36 hours; I knew I didn't dare to eat or drink anything—I knew I *couldn't* pee. Larry Palmer remembers eating "that fatal piece of toast."

Just the other day, we were remembering it together. "It was plain toast," Larry said. "No butter, no jam—I didn't even finish it."

"And nothing to drink?" I asked him.

"Not a drop," Larry said.

(Lately, we're in the habit of getting together at least once a year. Larry Palmer is Professor of Law at Cornell Law School; one of his kids has just started wrestling.)

On the scales at East Providence, Palmer was a quarter-pound over 121. He'd been a sure bet to get as far as the semifinals, and maybe farther; his disqualification cost us valuable team points—as did my loss to East Providence's Pieranunzi, who was tougher at home than he was in the pit. In two years, Pieranunzi and I had wrestled four matches. I beat him once, we tied once, he beat me twice—both times in the tournament, where it counted most. All our matches were close, but that last time (in East Providence) Pieranunzi pinned me. Thus, the two times I was pinned at Exeter—my first match and my last—I was pinned by a New England Champion from Rhode Island. (Exeter failed to defend its New England team title in '61—our '60 team was arguably the best in Exeter history.)

Larry Palmer was stunned. He *couldn't* have eaten a half-pound piece of toast!

Coach Seabrooke was, as always, philosophic. "Don't blame yourself—you're probably just growing," Ted told him. Indeed, this proved to be the case. Larry Palmer was the Exeter team captain the following year, 1962, when he won the New England Class A title at 147 pounds. More significant than his 26-pound jump from his former 121-pound class, Palmer had also grown six inches.

It's clear to me now that Larry Palmer's famous piece of toast at Howard Johnson's didn't weigh half a pound. Larry's growth spurt doubtless began on the bus. We were so sorry for him when he didn't make weight that none of us looked closely enough at him; in addition to gaining a half-pound, Larry was probably two inches taller by the time he got to East Providence—we might have seen the difference, had we looked.

The Books I Read

In schools—even in good schools, like Exeter—they tend to teach the shorter books by the great authors; at least they begin with those. Thus it was *Billy Budd, Sailor* that introduced me to Melville, which led me to the library, where I discovered *Moby Dick* on my own. It was *Great Expectations* and *A Christmas Carol* that introduced me to Dickens, and (also in English classes) I read *Oliver Twist* and *Hard Times* and *A Tale of Two Cities*, which led me (out of class) to read *Dombey and Son* and *Bleak House* and *Nicholas Nickleby* and *David Copperfield* and *Martin Chuzzlewit* and *Little Dorrit* and *The Pickwick Papers*. I couldn't get enough of Dickens, although he presented a challenge to my dyslexia—to the degree that my schoolwork certainly suffered. It was usually the shorter books by the authors I loved that drew me to their longer books, which I loved more. Loving long novels plays havoc with going to school.

In an Exeter English class, I was "started" on George Eliot with *Silas Marner*, but it was *Middlemarch* that would keep me from finishing my math and Latin assignments. My father, the Russian scholar, wisely started me on Dostoyevsky with *The Gambler*, but it was *The Brothers Karamazov* that I read and reread with an all-consuming excitement. (My father started me on Tolstoy and Turgenev, too.)

George Bennett was the first person in my life to introduce me to contemporary literature; in addition to his duties as Chairman of the Exeter English Department, George was simply a great reader—he read everything. I was still at Exeter—this was about

10 years before my fellow Americans would "discover" Robertson Davies upon the publication of *Fifth Business*—when George Bennett urged me to read *Leaven of Malice* and *A Mixture of Frailties*. (*Tempest-Tost*, the first novel of *The Salterton Trilogy*, I wouldn't read until much later.) And, not surprisingly, it was reading Robertson Davies that led me to Trollope. (With all there was to read of Trollope, this doubtless caused further injury to my schoolwork.) It has been said many times that Robertson Davies is Canada's Trollope, but I think he is also Canada's Dickens.

Twenty years later, Professor Davies reviewed *The Hotel New Hampshire* (1981) for *The Washington Post*. It was such a likable and mischievous review—and by then I'd read everything of his—that I eventually journeyed to Toronto for the sole purpose of having lunch with him. I'd broken a big toe (wrestling), and the toe was so swollen that none of my shoes would fit. My son Colin already had bigger feet than mine (by the time he was 16); yet it was only a pair of Colin's *wrestling shoes* that permitted me to walk without hobbling. It was either wear the wrestling shoes or meet Robertson Davies in my bare feet.

Professor Davies took me to the York Club in Toronto for a rather formal lunch; he was exceedingly polite and kind to me, but when his glance fell upon the wrestling shoes, his glance was stern. Now my wife, Janet, is his literary agent. Janet and I live part time in Toronto, where we dine frequently with Rob and Brenda Davies. Footwear is never a topic of conversation between us, yet I don't doubt that Professor Davies's memory of our first meeting remains somewhat critical.

When Janet and I were married in Toronto, my two sons from my first marriage, Colin and Brendan, were my best men, and Robertson Davies read from the Bible. Rob brought his own Bible to the wedding service, not trusting the Bishop Strachan Chapel to have the correct translation. (Professor Davies is a great defender of the King James Version in these treacherous modern times.)

Colin and Brendan had not met Rob before the wedding, and Brendan—he was 17 at the time—didn't see Professor Davies, in his magnificent white beard, approach the pulpit. Brendan looked up and, suddenly, there was this big man with a big beard and a bigger voice. Colin, who was 22 at the time, told me that Brendan looked as if he'd seen a ghost. But Brendan, who was not overly familiar with churches of any kind, had had a different thought. Brendan was quite certain that Professor Davies was God.

In addition to providing me with my first opportunity to read Robertson Davies—at a time when I was about the age Brendan was at my second wedding—George Bennett encouraged me to go beyond my initial experience with Faulkner. I don't remember *which* Faulkner novel I was introduced to (in an Exeter English class), but I struggled with it; I was either too young or my dyslexia rebelled at the length of those sentences, or both. I would never love Faulkner, or Joyce, but I grew to like them. And it was George who talked me through my earliest difficulties with Hawthorne and Hardy, too; I would grow to love Hardy, and Hawthorne— more than Melville—remains my favorite American writer. (I was never a Hemingway or Fitzgerald fan, and Vonnegut and Heller mean much more to me than Twain.)

It was also George Bennett who forewarned me that in all probability I would be "cursed to read like a writer," by which he meant that I would suffer from inexplicably strong and inexpressibly personal opinions; I think George really meant that I was doomed, like most of the writers I know, to have indefensible taste, but George was too generous to tell me that.

I can't read Proust, or Henry James; reading Conrad almost kills me. *The Rover* is okay, but most suitable for young males (under 18). *Heart of Darkness* is simply the longest short novel I know. I agree with one of Conrad's unkind reviewers that Marlow is "a garrulous intermediary"—I would call Marlow a tedious narrative device—and the same reviewer points out why I prefer (to *all* the rest) *The Rover*, which is generally looked down upon as Conrad's only children's book. "As nowhere else in Conrad," says the unkind reviewer, "disquisitions on ethics and psychology and metaphysics are conspicuously absent."

Not all "disquisitions" on such subjects are unbearable to me. It was *Death in Venice* that led me to the rest of Thomas Mann—particularly to *The Magic Mountain*, which I have read too many times to count. The literature of the German language wouldn't attract me with full force until I was in university, where I first read Goethe and Rilke and Schnitzler and Musil; they would lead me to Heinrich Böll and Günter Grass. Grass, García Márquez, and Robertson Davies are my three favorite living authors; when you consider that they are all comic novelists, for whom the 19th-century tradition of storytelling—of narrative momentum

and developed characters—remains the model of the form, I suppose you could say that I haven't ventured very far from Dickens.

With one exception: Graham Greene. Greene was the first
contemporary novelist I was assigned to read at Exeter; it would
probably have provoked him to know that I read him not in an
English class but in the Reverend Frederick Buechner's extremely
popular course on Religion and Literature. I took every course
Fred Buechner taught at Exeter, not because he was the school
minister but because he was the academy's only published novelist—and a good one. (I wouldn't realize *how* good until, long after
Exeter, I read Buechner's quartet of Bebb novels—*Lion Country*,
Open Heart, *Love Feast*, and *Treasure Hunt*.)

We were a negative lot of students at Exeter, when it came to
religion. We were more cynical than young people today; we were
even more cynical than most of us have since become—that is
to say that my generation strikes me as *less* cynical today than
we were. (Is that possible?) Anyway, we didn't like Freddy Buechner for his sermons in Phillips Church or in our morning chapel,
although his sermons were better than anyone else's sermons I've
ever heard or read—before or since. It was his eloquence about
literature that moved us; and his enthusiasm for Graham Greene's
The Power and the Glory, which engendered my enthusiasm for all
(or almost all) of Greene, was unstoppable.

I feel that I know Greene's people better than I know most
of the people I have known in my life, and they are not even
people I wanted (or would ever want) to know: it is that simple. I

cannot sit in the dentist's chair without envisioning the terrible Mr. Tench, the expatriate dentist who witnesses the execution of the whiskey priest. It is not Emma Bovary who epitomizes adultery to me: it is poor Scobie in *The Heart of the Matter*, and poor Scobie's awful wife, Louise; it is Helen, the 19-year-old widow with whom Scobie has an affair, and the morally empty intelligence agent, Wilson, who is a little bit in love with Louise. And then there is the ghastly sleaziness of *Brighton Rock:* the utterly corrupted 17-year-old Pinkie, and the innocent 16-year-old Rose . . . the murder of Hale, and Ida drinking stout. They have become what an "underworld" means to me, just as *The End of the Affair* is the most chilling antilove story I know. Poor Maurice Bendrix! Poor Sarah and poor Henry, too! They are like people you would shy away from if you encountered them on the street, knowing what you know.

"Hatred seems to operate the same glands as love: it even produces the same actions," Greene wrote. I used to have that typed on a yellowing piece of paper, taped to my desk lamp, long before I understood how true it was. Something I understood sooner—as soon as I began to write—is this cutting I also made from *The End of the Affair:* "So much of a novelist's writing . . . takes place in the unconscious: in those depths the last word is written before the first word appears on paper. We remember the details of our story, we do not invent them."

The End of the Affair is the first novel that shocked me. I read it at a time when most of my contemporaries (those who read at all) were being shocked by *The Catcher in the Rye*, which I thought was as perfunctory as masturbation. Salinger's familiar creation, that troubled boy, knew nothing that could compare to Bendrix's frightening knowledge that "there is no safety anywhere: a humpback, a cripple—they all have the trigger that sets love off."

Later, to think of Greene making the disclaimers he made—or describing some of his work, as he did, as mere "entertainments"—was confounding to me. Greene's manipulations of popular though "lesser" forms (the thriller, the detective story) obviously cost him the critical appreciation that is withdrawn from writers with too many readers.

I am reminded of Maurice Bendrix thinking of one of his critics. "Patronizingly in the end he would place me: probably a little above Maugham because Maugham is popular and I have not yet committed that crime, not yet; but although I retain a little of the exclusiveness of unsuccess, the little reviews, like wise detectives, can scent it on its way." Greene wrote this about Bendrix in 1951; Greene himself was already becoming popular—he would soon commit "that crime"—and the "wise detectives" would sniff at his success and bestow their praise on far less perfect craftsmen than Greene.

If, in the beginning—when I first read him in prep school—Graham Greene showed me that exquisitely developed characters and heartbreaking stories were the obligations of any novel worth remembering, it was also Greene, later, who taught me to loathe literary criticism; to see how the critics would dismiss him made me hate critics. Until his death, in 1991, Graham Greene was the most accomplished living novelist in the English language; in any language, he was the most meticulous.

As Greene was always keen to observe: coincidence is everywhere. Greene's niece, Louise Dennys, is my Canadian publisher. The man who introduced me to Greene, the Reverend Frederick Buechner—no longer the school minister at Exeter—is my old friend and neighbor in Vermont. (Small world.) And it is only mildly astonishing to me that by the time I left Exeter I had already read most of the writers who would matter to me in my life as a writer; it is also true that the hours I spent reading them contributed (in combination with my dyslexia) to the necessity of my spending a fifth year at a four-year school.

It hardly matters now. And it's a good lesson for a novelist: keep going, move forward—but slowly. Why be in a hurry to finish school, *or* a book?

A Backup

While the intelligentsia of my Exeter classmates moved on to various Ivy League colleges, or to their elite equivalents—George Trow moved slightly south to Harvard, where Larry Palmer would go the following year, and Chuck Krulak was accepted at the Naval Academy (Krulak had left Exeter for Annapolis the previous year)—I attended the University of Pittsburgh because I wanted to wrestle with the best.

I would have been happier at Wisconsin, where I was wait-listed for admission because I wasn't in the top quarter of my graduating class. (It's questionable that, if I'd gone to Exeter High School instead of the academy, I *would* have been, although this was my feeling at the time.) Rather than wait for Wisconsin to accept me, I chose Pitt. Why? Because Pittsburgh didn't make me wait.

I made a mistake. I liked George Martin, the Wisconsin wrestling coach, and he liked me; his son Steve, a future 157-pounder for Wisconsin, had been a teammate of mine (and a close friend) at Exeter. When I visited Madison, I loved the place—I loved the Badger wrestling room, too. Had I attended the University of Wisconsin, I might never have been a place winner in the Big 10 tournament—or even a starter on the Wisconsin team—but I know that I would have kept wrestling, and I would have stayed four years (maybe longer) in Madison; there's no question that I would have graduated. But I was 19—Pittsburgh had accepted me, and Wisconsin had told me to wait and see. When you're 19, you don't want to "wait and see."

Coach Seabrooke warned me that I might be getting in over my head at Pitt; I should go to a smaller school, I should try a less competitive wrestling program—these were Ted's recommendations. But when he couldn't persuade me, he wrote to Rex Peery, the coach at Pittsburgh, giving Rex his evaluation of me. Knowing Ted, I presume he didn't exaggerate my potential. Coach Peery was prepared for me to be no better than "halfway decent"; as it turned out, I was worse than that.

Rex Peery was an Oklahoma boy and a former three-time national champion—even his *sons* had been three-time NCAA champions—and Pittsburgh was loaded with future All-Americans the year I arrived. Dick Martin, the 123-pounder, would be an All-American; Darrel Kelvington (147) and Timothy Gay (157) and Jim Harrison (167) and Kenneth Barr (177) would also be All-Americans. (Harrison was a future national champion; he would win an NCAA title in 1963.) Then there were Zolikoff at 137 and Jeffries at 191 and Ware at Unlimited—I once could recite that lineup in my sleep.

Sherman Moyer, the Pitt 130-pounder and my most frequent workout partner, was married and had completed his military service. Sherm was reputed to smoke one cigarette a week—usually in a toilet stall before his match (at least this was the only place I ever *saw* him smoke)—and he was devastating in the top position. Sherman Moyer was simply impossible to get away from; he could ride me, and did, all afternoon. At the time, it was small consolation to me that Moyer's abilities as a "rider" led him to defeat Syracuse All-American Sonny Greenhalgh twice in that season. (Sonny and I still talk about Moyer.) Nor was it greatly consoling that Moyer was a gentleman; he was always decent and good-humored to me—ever friendly—while grinding me into the mat.

As for my fellow freshmen at Pitt, they were a tough lot, too—especially in and around my weight class. Tom Heniff was from Illinois and Mike Johnson was from Pennsylvania; they were often my workout partners—and Moyer's. Heniff and I were 130-pounders—I had dropped three pounds from my Exeter weight class—and

Johnson, who wrestled at 123 and at 130, could take apart anyone in the wrestling room up to about 140 or 150 pounds. In the next year, Mike Johnson would be an All-American; he was an NCAA runner-up in '63. (Johnson is a high-school wrestling coach in Du Bois, Pennsylvania, today.)

I also worked out with a couple of freshman 137-pounders: a redhead named Carswell or Caswell, who was pound for pound the strongest person I ever wrestled—I remember him as about five feet five with a 60-inch chest—and a smiling guy named Warnick who had an arm-drag that left you looking for your arm. The freshman recruit at 147 pounds was (I believe) a guy named Frank O'Korn; I don't remember him well—I must have wrestled him only occasionally. At 157 pounds, John Carr had won a New England Interscholastic title as a PG at Cheshire. (Carr would transfer from Pitt to Wilkes; until recently, he was a high-school coach in the Wilkes-Barre area of Pennsylvania.) And topping off that freshman class was a highly recruited 177-pounder named Lee Hall.

I knew they would be good—I had gone there because they were the best. But in the Pittsburgh wrestling room, in the '62 season, there was not one wrestler I could beat—not *one*.

My technique was not the problem; I had been well coached at Exeter. The problem in Pittsburgh was that my limited athletic ability placed me at a considerable distance from the top rank of college wrestlers around the nation. Because of Ted Seabrooke, I wasn't a bad wrestler; I also wasn't a good athlete, as Ted had told me. I took a pounding at Pitt. "Halfway decent" didn't cut it there.

I won't presume to define that essential ability which makes a "good athlete" for all sports, but for wrestling good balance is as important as quickness; it is also as uncoachable. And by balance I mean both kinds: the ability to keep your balance—to a small degree this can be taught, by maintaining good position—and how quickly you can recover your balance when you lose it. The latter ability is unteachable. The speed with which I can recover my balance when I lose it is mournfully slow; this is my weakness as an athlete. (It is a sizable limitation for a wrestler.)

In '62, freshmen were ineligible for varsity competition; yet I'd anticipated a challenging schedule of dual-meet matches and tournaments for the Pittsburgh freshman team—we would have been a winning team. But Johnson and Heniff and Warnick and O'Korn and Carr were either academically ineligible or nursing injuries, or both; what there was for a freshman wrestling schedule was canceled. The *only* competition I would see, until the year-end tournament—the Freshman Eastern Intercollegiates at West Point—was the considerable competition in the Pitt wrestling room. And I could easily predict my future, if I stayed at Pittsburgh. I would be a backup to Johnson or Heniff or Warnick (or to all three); later, I would be a backup to whatever talented freshmen would enter *next* year's wrestling room with the new freshman class. I would *always* be a backup. When one of the starters was sick, when he was hurt or couldn't make weight, I would sneak into the lineup; and there was little doubt what my role would be then—it wouldn't be to win but to not get pinned. It would be, at best, a career spent facing Vincent Buonomano—like my first time in the pit.

It was what success I had met with in the pit—*after* the beating by Buonomano—that made the backup role hard for me to bear. At Exeter, I had been a three-year starter. Years later, as a coach, I had the highest respect for the backup wrestlers on good wrestling teams; they were what made the teams good—*as teams*. They were the necessary workout partners who could have been starters at a smaller school, in a less competitive program. But once I'd been part of a program like Pittsburgh's, I couldn't have been satisfied with anything less; nor was I wise enough to recognize the distinction of backing up a wrestler of Mike Johnson's quality. Instead, I was disappointed in myself—in my limitations. I wanted to leave Pittsburgh, but there was nowhere else I wanted to go.

For once I was not struggling academically; yet, for the first time, I was lazy (academically), too. I worked hard in the wrestling room, but—without any outside competition—I couldn't see my own improvement as a wrestler. I could only see that I wasn't improving against Moyer or Johnson or Heniff or Warnick, or Carswell or Caswell—whatever the strong redhead's name was. And I was bored with everything *but* the wrestling; to simply *see* more of it—since I couldn't compete—I asked Coach Peery to take me on varsity road trips as the team manager. Rex took me; he knew I was discouraged, and he was being kind to me—I was an easily distracted manager. (Daydreamers have pathetic managerial skills.)

Rex Peery was always kind to me, except once when he cut my hair. We were traveling—we were in the training room at either

Navy or Maryland—and he'd warned me earlier to get a haircut.
I wasn't being in the slightest rebellious; I'd just forgotten to do
it—I would have done anything to please Rex.

Coach Peery put a surgical basin on my head—it was a bowl,
but not a round one—and he cut my hair with a pair of snub-
nosed shears, of the kind used for removing adhesive tape from
injured ankles and knees and shoulders and wrists and fingers . .
. and whatever else could be taped. (By the end of a wrestling season, almost everything was taped.) All things considered, it wasn't
a bad haircut—Rex would never try to make anyone look foolish.
Besides, emblematic of my experience at Pitt, I had brought the
haircut on myself.

The Hundred-Dollar Taxi Ride

It was about that time when I started smoking—just a little
bit, although a little more than Sherman Moyer. Maybe Moyer
had inspired me; if I couldn't get out from under him on the
mat, at least I could outsmoke him. It was a stupid way to try
to say good-bye to wrestling, which I wouldn't say goodbye to
until I was 47—whereas I would quit smoking almost as soon as
I started. Most self-destructive behavior is simply ridiculous—
never mind how complexly compelled by personal demons.
Given my limited talent, I could ill afford to undermine one of

my few advantages as a wrestler—before I started smoking, I was in fanatically good shape.

A pack would last me at least a week, often two weeks; and the more I smoked, the *harder* I trained. What was the point of it? So little smoking hardly constitutes an unbreakable habit—I'd never had the habit. In Pittsburgh, I could have used a school psychiatrist—and not for my spelling. In the back of my mind, even as I smoked, I imagined that I could redeem myself at the Freshman Eastern Intercollegiates; the three Pitt freshmen who were uninjured and eligible—I was one of them—would get to go.

It was probably because of my brief managerial experience that I was trusted with the bus tickets and pocket money for the trip to West Point; Coach Peery put me in charge. The varsity team was staying in Pittsburgh, preparing for the nationals; no coach would accompany Lee Hall and me, and Carswell or Caswell—I'm going to call him Caswell—to the tournament at Army. It seemed simple enough. I had bus tickets from Pittsburgh to the Port Authority in New York City, together with something called "transfer passes" from New York to West Point. I was told to get the three of us to Manhattan and take the first available bus up the Hudson. What could have been easier? But the bus from Pittsburgh was delayed; by the time we reached the Port Authority, it was midnight. The next available bus to West Point was at 8:00 in the morning; from filling out the registration forms from Army, I remembered that the weigh-ins were at 7:00 A.M.

"We can't miss the weigh-ins and still wrestle," Caswell said.

"What do we do?" Lee Hall asked me.

Inevitably, I recalled the surgical basin on my head—at either Navy or Maryland—and I wondered what Rex Peery would have wanted us to do. The whole year the three of us had been wrestling only our teammates in the wrestling room; it wouldn't have been like missing one tournament—it would have meant missing our *only* tournament. I counted the pocket money that Coach Peery had given me: $100. I had our return "transfer passes" from West Point to the Port Authority, and our return tickets from New York to Pittsburgh. All we had to do was get ourselves up the Hudson to West Point before 7:00 in the morning. What did we need the $100 for? (We had to make weight—we couldn't eat anything, anyway.)

Once outside the Port Authority—now it was well after midnight—I was glad to be in the company of our highly recruited 177-pounder, Lee Hall, and with Caswell, the pound-for-pound strongest person in the world. (Caswell would be wrestling at Army at 137 pounds. I was listed to weigh in at 130.) It took me a dozen cabs, or more, before I found a taxi driver who would take us to West Point for $100.

"West Point? A hundred bucks? Sure, man," the driver said. "Where's West Point?"

Caswell said he couldn't read a map in a moving car without throwing up, and Lee Hall couldn't comfortably fit in the front seat; the meter crowded him (Lee had to cut a lot of weight to weigh 177 pounds). Therefore, I was our navigator—I sat up front with the driver.

"You just go up the Hudson," I told him.

"Sure, man," he said. "Up the *what?*"

I have flown nonstop from New York to Tokyo; I have driven nonstop from Iowa City to Exeter, New Hampshire. But that trip up the Hudson was the longest of my life. Didn't the Dutch explore the Hudson in boats? Not even in a boat could we have made worse time.

In the first place, the only map was a map of Manhattan and Brooklyn and Queens and the Bronx. In the second place, as soon as the city lights were gone, our driver informed us that he was afraid of the dark.

"I never drove in the dark before," he whimpered. "Not *dis* dark!"

We inched along. It began to sleet. It seemed that only back roads led to West Point—at least they were the only roads we found.

"I never seen so many trees," our driver said. "Not *dis* many!"

If our taxi driver was terrified of the dark, and of the unusual number of trees, the soldiers who were dressed to kill—and who guarded the formidable entrance to the United States Military Academy at West Point (I presume they were M.P.s)—were his undoing. The Military Police were not expecting the predawn arrival of three wrestlers from Pittsburgh; the other wrestlers had long ago arrived—the soldiers presumed they'd gone to bed. However, it was not necessary to open our gym bags in order to verify that we were wrestlers; it was only necessary for the M.P.s to get a look at Lee Hall.

It was then a matter of deciding on the whereabouts of our

barracks. Where were all the other wrestlers sleeping? The soldiers at the gate, intimidating though they were, were not brave enough to call the Army wrestling coach and ask him where we were to be sheltered—it was about 4:00 A.M., only three hours to weigh-ins. Lee Hall and Caswell knew what I was thinking when I suggested to the soldiers that we sleep in the gym. I explained that the mats were usually rolled out the night before; that way the mats are lying flat by the time of competition—you don't have to tape the corners to the floor. We could sleep on the mats, I offered—we didn't mind.

Lee Hall and Caswell knew that I was thinking of the *scales*, not the mats—I couldn't have cared less about the mats, or sleeping. We had three hours before weigh-ins and we hadn't been able to check our weight since we left Pittsburgh. If I was a half-pound over, I needed to sweat; I'd been a pound and a half over when we left Pittsburgh. I'd eaten nothing, and I'd had nothing to drink; usually, if I was a pound and a half over in the afternoon before a morning weigh-in, I could drink eight ounces of water and still lose the weight in my sleep. I hadn't slept or had my usual eight ounces of water, but I was dying to get on the scales, to be sure.

The M.P.s didn't think that letting us into the gym was a good idea. There was a barracks somewhere for visiting teams; the soldiers sounded more or less sure of this, although they weren't sure which barracks it was.

Lee Hall confided to me that he thought we should go somewhere warm and "just run." That way we'd at least be losing weight.

And how much sleep would we get before weigh-ins, anyway? I agreed with Lee.

Caswell looked remarkably well rested; he'd slept the whole way from Manhattan and was now viewing the austere buildings of the military academy with the eagerness of a child who'd just arrived at an amusement park—apparently Caswell never worried about his weight.

It was then I noticed that our taxi driver was too frightened to leave; he couldn't possibly find his way back to the city—"not in *dis* dark," he said. The M.P.s were doubly unsure which barracks might be available for *him*.

One of the soldiers got up the nerve to make a phone call. I don't know the name or rank of the man who was awakened, but his voice was exceptionally powerful and loud. We were brought to a darkened building in a Jeep—our taxi driver, too; he'd happily left the keys to his cab with the M.P.s at the gate. It was one of those stone dormitories where the stairs were lit with timed lights; on each floor, a single switch turned on the lights for the entire stairwell. At every stair landing, next to the hall door, the light switch was indicated by a small bulb that glowed the dull yellow of a cat's eye. The lights "ticked" for two minutes and then they went out; to turn them on, you had to find the nearest cat's eye again. By this torturous method, a few wrestlers were sprinting or jogging up and down the stairs—sometimes in light, sometimes in darkness, depending on the whim of the timed lights in the stairwell. One of these stair runners directed us to a huge, bad-smelling, overheated room where many wrestlers were lying on cots; they were fully clothed, under mounds of blankets—trying to sweat off the extra weight while they slept. (Most of them were lying in the dark, awake.)

"Man, it stinks in here," our taxi driver said.

At first glance, it seemed there were no empty cots, but this didn't trouble Caswell, who made himself comfortable on top of his gym bag on the floor; I think he was asleep by the time Lee Hall and I had changed into our sweatsuits and were running around the stairwell. The guys who'd been running the stairs ahead of us had worked out a system with the lights: when the lights went out, whoever was nearest a stair landing looked for the dull-yellow bulb. We kept running, whether the lights were on or off. Nobody talked on the stairs. Every so often I would call out "Lee?" and Lee Hall would say "What?"

After 15 or 20 minutes, I was sweating the way I wanted to; I started trotting more slowly, moving just fast enough so the sweat didn't stop. I think I was asleep when I ran into a wall in the dark. My eyebrow was split open. I could feel that I was bleeding, but I didn't know how badly I was cut.

"Lee?" I called.

"What?" Lee Hall said.

* * *

A Thief

I was 128 pounds at the weigh-ins. The Army trainer shaved my eyebrow and covered the cut with a butterfly bandage; he advised me to have the cut stitched up properly when I got back to Pittsburgh. I knew I'd run too much—my legs felt dead.

We went to the mess hall after weigh-ins, and there was our taxi driver; it's time I gave him a name—let's call him Max.

"What are you doing here, Max?" I said. For starters, Max was eating an enormous breakfast—steeling his courage for the ride back to Manhattan, I thought. But Max had decided he'd hang around and watch the preliminary round of matches.

"If you guys win, maybe I'll stay for the next round," Max informed us. "Anyway, it's still sleeting." In the daylight, Max appeared to be almost erudite. It also seemed he had adopted us. We were trying to get focused on the tournament—we didn't give the matter of Max much thought. Lee Hall ate a much bigger breakfast than I did; my stomach was shrunk—I felt hungry but, after half a bowl of oatmeal, I felt full. Caswell, with his characteristic air of contentment, took a nap in the locker room after consuming a generous number of what looked like pancakes.

They were posting the brackets for the different weight classes on the walls of the gym, and Lee Hall and I looked over the matchups for 130 and 177 pounds. I wished Caswell hadn't been sleeping, because I wanted to drill some takedowns; Lee Hall and I were the wrong size to drill with each other. Instead, I rolled around on the mats by myself and watched the crowd straggle in.

I remember it as an old, oval-shaped gym with a wooden track above, like an elongated version of the pit at Exeter, except that the floor space was vast; there were at least six mats rolled out for the preliminary rounds, and a long line of bleacher seats—extending almost to matside—ran the length of the gym wall.

I kept an eye out for my parents; although they were making a two-day trip of it—they had left New Hampshire yesterday and had spent the night with friends in Massachusetts—it wasn't like them to be late. Depending on the number of entries in your weight class, you might have two or three preliminary matches before the quarterfinal round, later that afternoon; the semifinals were that night. The next day would begin with the wrestle-backs (the consolation rounds), which would lead to the consolation finals; the finals would be tomorrow afternoon. It would be dark by the time we got to New York, I was thinking—and a long night's ride on the bus back to Pittsburgh. We would be hungry then, with no more weigh-ins to make—and no money for food. I was also thinking that it was odd to be at a big tournament without a coach.

With me wrestling 130, and Caswell at 137, we would often be wrestling on different mats at the same time, or at overlapping times; we wouldn't be able to coach each other—Lee Hall would have to choose between coaching me and coaching Caswell. As it turned out, when Lee Hall was wrestling, both Caswell and I were available to coach him. Lee, however, needed little coaching; he would easily maul his way into the finals—his opponents rarely lasted past the second period. Caswell and I would shout out the

time remaining on the clock; that was all Lee needed to know—
Lee didn't need to be informed of the lopsided score.

John Carr, our ineligible (or injured) 157-pounder, had not
made the trip to West Point, but his dad was there; Mr. Carr vol-
unteered to coach Caswell and Lee Hall and me. Mr. Carr loved
wrestling; he must have spent many exciting years watching his
son—John Carr was a very good wrestler. I remember thinking
that Mr. Carr must have been disappointed to be watching *me*. I
remember little else about the preliminary rounds. I beat two guys
from schools with monosyllabic names (like Pitt). I could guess
that they were from Yale and Penn, but they could have been from
anywhere; it doesn't matter—in both matches, I got the first takedown so cleanly that I kept repeating it.

You take the guy down, you're up two points; you let the guy
go, he gets one point—then you take him down again. After your
three takedowns and his three escapes, you're leading 6–3. After
that, the guy has to chase you, which makes it easier for you to
take him down.

I was working Warnick's arm-drag, which Warnick had
worked on me all winter in the Pitt wrestling room; I was working
a duck-under, although it wasn't nearly as smooth a duck-under as
Mike Johnson used to work on me—about a hundred times a week.
Anyway, I advanced to the quarterfinals, realizing that I'd actually
learned a little wrestling in the course of taking a pounding at Pitt.

In the quarterfinals, I pinned a guy from R.P.I.—I remember
where he was from only because Lee Hall or Caswell asked me

what "R.P.I." stood for and I realized that I didn't know how to spell Rensselaer *or* Polytechnic. Suddenly I was in the semifinals.

That hour—maybe it was two or three hours—between the quarterfinals and the semifinals . . . that was the best time of my one season of wrestling at Pittsburgh. That was when I knew I wasn't coming back. Lee Hall was talking to me; he was saying what a great freshman team we had—if only most of them had been able to wrestle. He was saying that Pitt would have walked away with the team title at that tournament—if only Johnson and Heniff and Warnick and O'Korn and Carr had been there. I agreed with Lee. But I knew that if Johnson and Heniff and Warnick and O'Korn and Carr had been there, I wouldn't have been wrestling; there was no room for me in that lineup. Caswell would have agreed with me: in such a lineup, there would have been no room for Caswell either.

And so I began to savor just being in the semifinals. It's fatal when you do that; you have to think about winning—not that you feel good to just *be* there. It's fatal to get distracted, too, and I was a little distracted; the thought that I would not come back to Pittsburgh had been in my mind before the Freshman Eastern Intercollegiates, of course—only now I *knew* it. I was also worried about my parents. Where were they?

I called their friends in Massachusetts, where they'd spent the previous night; to my surprise, my mother answered the phone. The sleet that was falling at West Point was snow in New England. My mom and dad had to wait out the storm. Whether I won or lost in the semifinals, I would be wrestling the next day—either in the finals or in the consolation matches that could lead to a third or a fourth-place finish. My parents would see me wrestle at West Point tomorrow, either way. It was a long trip for them, from New Hampshire; they'd never missed a match of mine at Exeter, and I began to feel a little pressure—to win for *them*. That's fatal, too—the wrong kind of pressure is fatal. You have to want to win for *you*.

I *wasn't* distracted by the discovery that Max, our taxi driver, was nowhere to be seen; he might not have been as interested in watching us wrestle as he'd claimed. It was later that evening when I learned that some of my fellow wrestlers had been robbed; they'd left their wallets or their wristwatches in the locker room, either forgetting or neglecting to put that kind of stuff in the team's "valuables box." I immediately suspected Max. In retrospect, I thought he had the perfect combination of instant charm and compulsive deceit that I associate with thieves; yet his terror of the night, and of the multitude of trees, could never have been feigned—not unless I have underestimated his thespian skills.

The Semifinals

As for the semifinals, I was what Coach Seabrooke always said I was—I was "halfway decent"—but the other guy was good. He was a kid from Cornell, and the favorite to win the weight class; he was the number-one seed. In the absence of a coach who knew me—Mr. Carr, given the greater abilities of his own son, generously overestimated my potential—I wrestled the kind of careful match that Ted Seabrooke would have recognized as the only kind of match I could win against a better wrestler. I even got the first takedown. But the Cornell kid escaped immediately—I couldn't manage to hold him long enough to gain any riding-time advantage—and he scored a slick takedown at the edge of the mat, just as time was running out in the first period; I had no time to get an escape of my own. I was trailing 3–2 going into the second period, and the choice of position (a flip of the coin) was mine; I chose down. I finally escaped for a point, but the Cornell kid had ridden me for over a minute. It was 3–3 on the scoreboard but I knew he had a riding-time point, which made it 4–3 in his favor starting the third—unless I could keep him on the bottom long enough to erase his riding-time advantage. He got away from me in less than 15 seconds, which made it 4–3 on the scoreboard—in reality, 5–3 (with riding time). I knew that the two-point difference was a *possible* gap for me to close in the final period.

Then I got lucky: my butterfly bandage was soaked through—my eyebrow was bleeding on the mat. The referee called a time-out to wipe up the blood, and I was given a quick rebandaging. However few cigarettes I'd been smoking, I was tired; it's not unreasonable to blame my tiredness on my lack of sleep, or on a dawn spent running up and down the stairs (into a wall)—but I blame the cigarettes. The mainstay of what had made me "halfway decent" as a wrestler was my physical conditioning; now a time-out for bleeding had given me a much-needed rest. (In those days, a college wrestling match was nine minutes long; in prep school,

I had been used to six minutes. A three-minute period feels a *lot* longer than a two-minute period. Nowadays, a college match is only seven minutes overall—divided in periods of three, two, two—and the high-school or prep-school match is what it always was: six minutes, in periods of two, two, two.)

And I got lucky again: the referee hit the Cornell wrestler with a warning for stalling. It was a questionable call. With the score 4–3 on the scoreboard (5–3 with riding time), I knew that a takedown could tie it; a takedown could win it for me, too—if I could stay on top long enough to negate his riding-time advantage. The stalling warning against my opponent would hurt him in a tie; in the rules of that tournament, there was no overtime, no sudden death—a draw would mean a referee's decision. I was sure that my opponent's warning for stalling would give any referee's decision to me—I thought a tie would win it.

I don't remember my takedown—whether it was Warnick's arm-drag or Johnson's duck-under, or whether it was a low, outside single-leg, which was my best takedown from Exeter—but there were less than 20 seconds showing on the clock, and the scoreboard said 5–4 in my favor. The Cornell kid had the riding-time point locked up—I couldn't erase his advantage in less than 20 seconds— and so the match would be a draw, 5–5, *if* I could just hold on.

There was a scramble, a mix-up of the kind that Coach Seabrooke had warned me against; fortunately, for me, we both rolled off the mat. When the referee brought us back to the circle, there were 15 seconds on the clock; I had to ride him for only 15 seconds. This is a drill in every practice session in every wrestling room in

America. Sometimes the drill is called "bursts." One of you tries to hang on, the other one tries to get away.

I don't remember how my opponent escaped, but he got free in a hurry. I had less than five seconds to initiate a desperation shot at a takedown; I wasn't close to completing a move when the buzzer sounded—I lost 6–5. I couldn't bear watching the Cornell kid in the finals; I don't know if he won the weight class or not—or, as I say so often, I don't remember. All I know is, that kid would never have gotten away from Sherman Moyer—not even in 15 *minutes*.

Point by point, move by move, you never know how close you are to getting into the finals of a tournament until you *don't* get into the finals. I called my parents in Massachusetts and told them to be at West Point early in the morning; the consolation rounds would start early. If I lost my first consolation match, I'd be eliminated from the tournament—I'd be a spectator for the rest of the day. If I won, I could keep wrestling; I could place as high as third, if I kept winning.

My next opponent was an Army boy—a home-crowd favorite of the West Point fans. I remember all those cadets in gray, leaning over the mats from the wooden track above the gym; I remember them screaming. It was a larger teacup than the pit at Exeter, but it was the same teacup effect—except that these were *his* fans, not mine. I'd wrestled as good a match as I could against the Cornell kid. Possibly it was the effect of the cadets, or maybe I was trying to impress my parents with everything I'd learned at Pitt; for whatever reason, my match against Army was not the kind of match Ted Seabrooke would have recommended for me. It was one mix-up after another; it was all a scramble. I knew from the beginning that I wouldn't win a free-for-all.

To be fair to myself, I not only lost the first takedown but I was thrown to my back and lost three points for a near-fall in addition to the takedown points. When I reversed him, I was still behind 5–2; he immediately reversed me, and I immediately escaped. When I had a second to look at the score, I saw I was losing 7–3 and the first period had just started. You can't slow down the pace when you're losing 7–3, and so that was the kind of match I was in—a free-for-all. I kept scoring, but he kept scoring back; whenever I checked the score, I was always no more than 5 but no fewer than 3 points behind. The cadets were screaming, not only because their West Point boy was winning; it was the kind of match a crowd loves—*any* crowd loves a free-for-all. I don't remember the final score: 15–11, 17–13. . . . Ted Seabrooke would have told me—indeed, Ted *had* told me—that I would *never* come out on top of a score like that. It was my last match in a Pittsburgh uniform, which I had worn for all of two days.

Whether they were disappointed or merely underimpressed, my parents were kind enough not to say. My mother was shocked to see how thin I was. I'd gotten much stronger in the wrestling room at Pitt, but I was nonetheless smaller than I'd been at Exeter; unlike Larry Palmer, I'd stopped growing when I was 15. My mom was worried about my weight. To that end, I was able to get some money from her—so that Caswell and Lee Hall and I could eat all the way back to Pittsburgh. I don't think I told my parents about the hundred-dollar taxi ride; I know I didn't tell them that

I'd made up my mind to leave Pitt—I still didn't know where I would go.

I don't even remember if Lee Hall won the Freshman Easterns or if he lost in the finals; it wasn't like Lee to lose, but I vaguely recall that he had a difficult opponent—a Lehigh kid, as I remember him, but I'm on record for not remembering much. For example, I don't remember how Caswell did; in the end, like me, I think he won a couple of matches and lost a couple—I know he didn't make the finals, but he might have placed. (Caswell did everything in such a friendly, efficient, uncomplaining way; that's probably why I can't even be sure of his name.)

Back in Pittsburgh, I will never forget telling Coach Peery that I'd spent all the pocket money.

"You took a *taxi*?" Rex kept saying.

I had so much respect for Rex I couldn't tell him why I was leaving Pitt: specifically because I couldn't bear being a backup. Instead, I made up a story about missing a girlfriend back home; I thought this sounded more human—hence more forgivable. I didn't have a girlfriend "back home," or in Pittsburgh.

My *ex*-girlfriend was from Connecticut; she was spending the year in Switzerland. The only Creative Writing I'd managed to do at Pitt was a diary I kept; I was imagining that I would show my ex-girlfriend my diary—and thus win her back. Everything in the "diary" was made up; I hadn't exactly had the kind of year that made me want to write about it. I didn't know this at the time, but I had begun a traditional writer's task—namely, I was in the process of inventing myself. Before I could invent anything else, I needed to practice.

A Brief Conversation in Ohio

In Pittsburgh—notwithstanding my disappointment in my wrestling—it had been a defeat of a deeper kind to be abused in Freshman English, where I received the grade of C– and was told by an instructor with less of a beard to shave than my own that my overuse of the semicolon was archaic. I shall call him Instructor C–, and if he is reading me still, which would surprise me, there is no telling what he makes of my semicolons today; if they were archaic in 1962, they must be antiquated beyond redemption now.

But I stopped neither writing nor wrestling as a result of these discouragements. I retreated to my home state of New Hampshire, not necessarily to lick my wounds. Even with my unimpressive grades at Pitt, the University of New Hampshire was obliged to admit me because of my in-state residency, and it was there that I took my first Creative Writing class by name. The teacher was a Southern novelist named John Yount—an engaging, good-humored, and good-hearted man who didn't bat an eye at my semicolons.

At the same time I became an extra coach in the wrestling room at Exeter, and I competed "unattached" in various "open" wrestling tournaments around New England and New York State; the University of New Hampshire had no wrestling team.

The competition in so-called open tournaments was a mixed bag: some of the entries were the better, more mature high-school wrestlers; there were lots of college freshmen and nonstarters on college teams; and always a few older, postcollege competitors— some of these wrestlers were very good, often the best in such tournaments, but others were . . . well, *too* old, or simply out-of-shape. I was in halfway-decent shape—not in Pittsburgh shape, but this wasn't Pittsburgh.

Although I was not attached to any team, I competed in my old Exeter uniform—with Ted Seabrooke's blessing. For take-downs, I had fair success with Warnick's arm-drag and Johnson's duck-under and with my own low, outside single-leg; defensively, on my feet—in the neutral position—I had a pretty good whizzer. Sherman Moyer had taught me the value of hand control; on top, I was hard to get away from but I was no pinner, and on the bottom I was difficult to hold down—although Moyer had managed to ride me until the clock ran out.

In lieu of cutting weight, I started *lifting* weights: if I couldn't make the cut to the 130-pound class, I would make myself strong enough to wrestle at 137 or 147. (In the open tournaments, the weight classes varied between collegiate and freestyle—sometimes I wrestled at 136½ or 137, other times at 147 or 149½.) A factor in what I weighed was beer; I turned 21 in the middle of the '63 wrestling season—at about the same time I gave up cigarettes, I took up beer.

Not surprisingly, the writers (and would-be writers) at the University of New Hampshire all smoked and drank; that I drove 45 minutes every day from Durham to Exeter for wrestling practice, and that I traveled on many weekends to wrestling tournaments, struck both me and my new writer friends as exceedingly unliterary. It was my earliest indication that my writing friends and my wrestling friends would rarely mix; for a brief period of time, I would give up the mixture myself—I was convinced that I could be a wrestler *or* a writer, but not both.

That March of '63, Ted Seabrooke and I drove out to Kent State University in Ohio to see the NCAA tournament. From the stands, I watched my old teammates at Pitt become All-Americans: Jim Harrison won the championship, Mike Johnson lost in the finals, Timothy Gay placed fifth, and Kenneth Barr was sixth. (I believe that the NCAA Division I tournament is the toughest in wrestling; it is both mentally and physically a tougher tournament than the Olympics—first of all, because of the tremendous pressure college wrestlers put on themselves to become All-Americans, but also because of how evenly matched many of the competitors are. In the 1995 tournament, there were six returning national champions; only two of them managed to defend their titles—and, out of 10 weight classes, only four of the number-one seeds finished first.)

A year away from Pittsburgh, I saw how far I stood from the top level of competition; it depressed me—I was 21, but I felt I'd failed at the one thing I'd been any good at. Worse than "failed"—I had *quit*. On our way home from Kent State, Ted told me that he'd talked with my Pitt coach, Rex Peery; Rex had been kind to me, as always—he had expressed his hope to Ted that I'd solved my "girlfriend problem."

"*What* 'girlfriend problem'?" Ted asked me.

I had to confess to Coach Seabrooke that I'd lied to Coach Peery about my reasons for leaving Pittsburgh. Mike Johnson had just finished second in the nation; yet I'd quit the Pitt team because I couldn't accept the role of spending four years as Johnson's workout partner. Far less honorable than being a backup to Mike Johnson was that I'd lied to Rex—I had made up a girlfriend, of all things.

"Johnny, Johnny," Ted Seabrooke said to me. (We were standing side by side at a urinal, still in Ohio.) "You don't have to give up wrestling because you're not the best wrestler," Ted told me. "You can still do it. And you're always going to love it—you can't help that."

But I didn't know that then. I had room in me to do, and to love, only what I thought I could be the best at, and John Yount had told me I could be a writer.

"So do it," Coach Seabrooke said.

It was Ted's idea that I should get out of New Hampshire; that I shouldn't be living at home and hanging out in the wrestling room of my old school—that if I were going to give up wrestling, I should give up more than that. I should get away—*far* away. Pittsburgh, of course, had been "away," but not far enough.

* * *

A Year Abroad

It was with John Yount's encouragement that I applied to a study-abroad program; as it turned out, the Institute for European Studies in Vienna admitted me. I went off to Europe feeling, for the first time, "like a writer."

I took 12 tutorial hours of German a week, but to this day I can speak the language only haltingly; I can barely understand German, when I'm spoken to, and reading German only serves to remind me of my dyslexia—all those verbs lurking at the end of the sentence, waiting to be reattached to the clauses they came from.

My favorite courses at the Institute for European Studies were taught by an Englishman named Edward Mowatt, with whom I studied (not necessarily in this order) Ludwig Josef Johann Wittgenstein and Greek Moral Philosophy. I also studied the Victorian Novel with Herr Doktor Felix Korninger from the University of Vienna. Professor Korninger was an Austrian who'd once taught at the University of Texas; he spoke English with a most original Texan-Austrian accent—a kind of conflation of Lyndon Baines Johnson and Arnold Schwartzenegger.

In Vienna, I shared an apartment on the Schwindgasse, next to the Polish Reading Room, with a fellow American named Eric Ross; he was from Chicago. Eric was tall and athletic, with honey-colored, curly hair; on skis, especially, he was a picture of Aryan perfection, but of course he was Jewish—and most savvy of the myriad, insidious forms of anti-Semitism in Austria. I knew nothing about anti-Semites, but I learned. I was short and dark and my last name was Irving—a Scots name, but common enough as a Jewish first name so that several Viennese anti-Semites were confused. (This is on a level of intelligence with thinking that John Milton was Jewish because of Milton Friedman, but—as Eric Ross was wise to point out—no one ever said anti-Semites were smart.) Eric and I developed a routine for exposing anti-Semites. Whether I was mistreated by a waiter or a shopkeeper, or by a fellow student at the University of Vienna, it was only necessary for the faintest hint of an anti-Semitic slur to emerge; I would not infrequently miss the slur—my German being as flawed as it was—but Eric, whose German was much better than mine, would instantly alert me to the insult.

"You're being treated like a Jew again," Eric would tell me.

Whereupon, pointing to Eric, I would deliver my well-rehearsed line to the offending anti-Semite: "*He's* the Jew, you idiot." ("*Er ist der Jude, Du Idiot.*") Eric always had to help me with the correct pronunciation, but we usually got our point across: Jew baiting was not merely distasteful—those with the inclination to do it were also stupid enough to think that they could tell who was Jewish and who wasn't.

Eric and I traveled to Istanbul together, and to Athens; we often went skiing together, too—in Kaprun. But while we both loved the experience of being on our own in Europe, we did not love—we *do* not love—Vienna. It is a small town; its notorious anti-Semitism is only part of a mean-spirited provincialism—an overall xenophobia, a suspicion (leading to hatred) of *all* outsiders.

"*Das gebt bei uns nicht,*" the Austrians say—"That doesn't go with us." "*Ausländer*"—a "foreigner"—is always a derogatory word. Viennese *Gemütlichkeit*, a tourist attraction, is the false sweetness of basically *unhöflich* people.

I was last in Vienna to promote the German translation of *A Prayer for Owen Meany,* and I got in trouble with the media for saying these things; at the time, the revelations about Kurt Waldheim's role in World War II appeared to have *enhanced* Waldheim's popularity in Vienna—and I said so. I doubt I'll go back to Vienna again.

When I was a student there, Freud's former apartment and office at 19 Berggasse was *not* open to the public; only the persistent efforts of Freud's daughter finally forced the Austrian government to let the modest *Wohnung* at 19 Berggasse stand for what it is: a most moving museum of an intellectual life interrupted by Nazi doctrine.

Freud was not mistaken to call Arthur Schnitzler a "colleague" in the study of the "underestimated and much-maligned erotic"; in my student days, this was doubtless the source of my fondness for Schnitzler—the "underestimated and much-maligned erotic," which Schnitzler often juxtaposed with the oppressive but slowly changing social order of fin-de-siècle Vienna. But even *The Road into the Open* (1908) was steeped in the *same* sexually oppressive atmosphere that Eric Ross and I would encounter in Vienna more than half a century later.

Observe young Baron Georg von Wergenthin looking out a window. "Outside, the park was rather empty. On a bench sat an old woman wearing an outmoded coat with black glass pearls. A governess walked by, a little boy on her hand, and another person, much smaller and in a hussar's uniform, with his saber buckled on and a pistol at his side, walked ahead, looked proudly around himself, and saluted an invalid who came down the path smoking. Deeper in the garden, around the kiosk, a few people sat drinking coffee and reading newspapers. The foliage was still rather thick, and the park seemed oppressed, dusty, and on the whole more summerlike than usual in late September." (Two pages later, young Georg is thinking about "the masquerade at the Ehrenbergs" and remembering "Sissy's fleeting kiss under the black lace of her mask.")

True, the small man in the hussar's uniform with his saber and pistol was gone from the Stadtpark by the time Eric Ross and I arrived in Vienna, but the "oppressed" atmosphere was largely unchanged. Eric and I used to study in the evenings in a bar where the prostitutes waited for their customers out of the cold. Our landlady turned off the heat at night, and the coffeehouses frequented by students were too noisy for studying; besides, the Viennese students were too proper to be seen in a bar used by prostitutes—except for the one or two well-to-do students who would appear at the bar in order to *select* a prostitute. (These students were always embarrassed to be seen by Eric or me.) As for the prostitutes, they recognized from the beginning that Eric and I could not afford their more intimate company. Occasionally, there was an older one—my mother's age—who would help me with my German.

Baron von Wergenthin might first have attracted my interest

in *The Road into the Open* because of his ceaseless fantasizing about women—and the ongoing difficulty of his relationships with them—but young Georg was also a Christian aristocrat whose principal friendships were with Jewish intellectuals, at a time when anti-Semitism was on the rise. By the time Eric Ross and I arrived in Vienna, anti-Semitism had not only risen, it had arrived—and it was intractable. It was also much more vulgar than my encounters with it in Schnitzler.

Witness Georg's meeting with Willy Eissler in the Stadtpark. It is *subtly* uncomfortable how Willy defends his Jewishness. He says: "The fact that I once had differences with Captain Ladisc cannot keep me from observing that he's always been a drunken pig. I have an insurmountable revulsion, irredeemable even by blood, against people who associate with Jews when it's to their advantage, but who begin to revile them as soon as they're outside on the steps. One could at least wait until one got to the coffeehouse."

Later, Baron von Wergenthin reflects that "he found it almost strange, as he often had before, that Willy was Jewish. The older Eissler, Willy's father, composer of charming Viennese waltzes and songs, distinguished art and antique collector and sometime dealer, with his giant's physique, had been known in his time as the foremost boxer in Vienna, and, with his long, full, gray beard and monocle, resembled more a Hungarian magnate than a Jewish patriarch. But talent, dilettantism, and an iron will had given Willy the affected image of a born cavalier. But what really distinguished him from other young people of his background and aspirations was the fact that he was content not to renounce his heritage; he pursued an explanation or reconciliation for every ambiguous smile, and in the face of pettiness or prejudice, by which he often appeared to be affected, he refused to make light of it whenever possible."

By the time Eric Ross and I arrived in Vienna, the anti-Semitism had long been administered by means more severe than the "ambiguous smile"; it had degenerated to base thuggery—it was impossible "to make light of it." Skinheads with swastika earrings, while not unusual, were not commonplace; what *were* commonplace were the shy citizens who looked away from the skinheads, pretending not to have seen them. As young, idealistic Americans, Eric and I could do no more than hold up a mirror to this inexplicable tolerance of intolerance. More than 30 years later, it is still a frequent topic of conversation between Eric and me: not simple intolerance but the tolerance of intolerance, which allows the intolerance to persist.

Eric Ross went into the advertising business in Chicago; then he moved to Crested Butte, Colorado, where he was a ski patrolman and a folk singer for many years. Eric still lives in Crested Butte, where he is a tireless contributor (both as an actor and a director) to the Crested Butte Mountain Theatre; and he's back writing ads again, when he's not writing letters to me—he's a most faithful correspondent. We try to see each other every year, together with our mutual best friend, David Warren. David is from Ithaca, New York—he was Eric's and my nearly constant companion in Vienna, and the best student among us.

Eric had the best motorcycle—a German Horex. However, the

Horex lacked a kickstand, which for reasons peculiar to Eric was never replaced; the Horex was always falling down. My motorcycle was second-best among our three: a Yugoslavian Jawa—or maybe it was Czech? And David drove a terrible Triumph; it was always dying on him—it preferred stranding him on the autobahn to other places.

Anyway, for no good reason—except that I had gotten away (*far* away) from New Hampshire—I started to write. I had Ted Seabrooke and John Yount to thank for the move.

It was also John Yount who encouraged me to stay in Europe, at a later time (that same year) when I was homesick; I was missing, among other things, both wrestling and a girlfriend who would become my first wife. I had met Shyla Leary in Cambridge in the summer of '63, just before I left for Vienna—I was taking a crash course in German at Harvard summer school. It seems idiotic, but I think it's fairly common that we meet people of importance to us just before we are going away somewhere. Within a year, in the summer of '64, I would marry her—in Greece.

"Stay in Europe for a while," Mr. Yount wrote to me. "Melancholy is good for the soul."

Surely this was good and true advice, and beyond the call of duty of Creative Writing teachers. I see now that John Yount was, if not my first mentor, the first *writer* I was conscious of as a mentor; he made a world of difference to me—largely by impressing upon me that anything I did except writing would be unsatisfying. Even so, I didn't take his advice—I didn't stay in Europe.

I had tried another language, and I was uncomfortable with

it; English was my *only* language, and—as a writer—I wanted it to be the language I lived with. Besides, Shyla and I had returned to Vienna from Greece—and she was already pregnant with Colin. I wanted to be a father, but only in my own country.

No Vietnam; No More Motorcyles

When I came back to the States, and to the University of New Hampshire, it was another writer who took me under his wing. Thomas Williams was much more to me than a teacher; his wife, Liz, would be the godmother of my first child, and Mr. Williams remained, until his death, my sternest and most passionate critic. Tom had a lifelong quarrel with my fondness for imitation—specifically, for imitating the narrative voices of many 19th-century novelists. He would not infrequently write in the margins of my manuscripts: "Who are you imitating now?" But his affection for me was genuine, as was mine for him; and his loyalty to me, when other critics would attack me, was steadfast. Tom Williams was a good friend, and it was on the strength of his reputation and his recommendation that I was given a teaching-writing fellowship to attend the Writers' Workshop at the University of Iowa. (Already married as an undergraduate, and with one child, I could not have afforded Iowa without the fellowship.) And it was Tom's agent who sold my first short story to *Redbook* for a whopping, at the time, $1,000. This sale occurred before I graduated from the University of New Hampshire, which caused me to be cordially loathed by my fellow students. But I was on my way to Iowa—what did I care?

That year in New Hampshire (my last) was a watershed for me. Not only did I become a published writer and a father, but the birth of my son Colin would change my draft status to 3A—"married with child"—which would forever isolate me from the dilemma facing my generation of American males; I would never have to make up my mind about Vietnam, because I couldn't be drafted. If Colin kept me out of Vietnam, the combination of being married and a father, *and* my return to the world of wrestling, kept me from experimenting with the most seductive hallmarks of my '60s generation: sex and drugs. I was a husband and a daddy and a jock—and, only recently, a writer.

I had just turned 23 when Colin was born. It was late March, which is not spring in New Hampshire. I remember driving my motorcycle home from the hospital. (A friend had driven Shyla to the hospital, because I'd been in class—in Tom Williams's Creative Writing class.) I remember watching out for the patches of ice and snow that were still evident on the roads; I drove home very slowly, put the motorcycle in the garage, and never drove it again—I would sell it that summer. It was a 750cc Royal Enfield, black and chrome, with a customized tomato-red gas tank the shape of a teardrop—I would never miss it. I was a father; fathers didn't drive motorcycles.

The night Colin was born, George Bennett died in the same hospital; I have called George my first "critic and encourager"— he was my first *reader.* I remember going back and forth in the hospital between Shyla and Colin and George. During the years I'd grown up in Exeter, especially before I attended the academy, George's son had been my best friend. (I would dedicate my first novel *in memory of* George, and to his widow and son.)

George Bennett took me to my first Ingmar Bergman film; it would have been 1958 or '59 when I saw *The Seventh Seal*—the movie was almost new (it was released in the U.S. in '57). It's not psychologically complicated why, when Death came for George, I saw Death as that relentless chess player in the black robe (Bengt Ekerot) who defeats the Knight (Max von Sydow) and claims the lives of the Knight's wife and the Knight's squire, too.

I have since read that *The Seventh Seal* is a "medieval fantasy," and this I don't understand at all . . . well, "medieval," maybe, although most of Bergman's work is timeless to me. But *The Seventh Seal* is no "fantasy." That Death takes the Knight and allows the young family to live . . . well, that was how it happened to me, too. At the moment my son Colin was born, George was gone.

In 1982, when Ingmar Bergman retired as a filmmaker—with *Fanny and Alexander*, the stunning memoir of his childhood—I felt another loss. Bergman was the only major novelist making movies. My interest in the movies, which was never great, has grown fainter since his retirement. I hope that Mr. Bergman is happy in the theater (where he continues to direct), although I have difficulty seeing him there—my interest in the theater was never great either.

* * *

Not Even a Zebra

Upon my return from Europe, Ted Seabrooke had made me feel welcome in the Exeter wrestling room, but something had changed in me; I was so happy to be wrestling again I didn't care how I compared to the competition—I didn't enter a single tournament. I worked out, hard, every day; I coached the kids at Exeter—I thought more about *their* wrestling than I did about mine—and I became certified as a referee. (I'd always disliked referees until I became one.)

That winter of '65, there was an additional wrestling coach in the Exeter room—a retired Air Force lieutenant colonel, Cliff Gallagher. Cliff was the famous Ed Gallagher's brother. (Between 1928 and 1940, E. C. Gallagher coached Oklahoma State to 11 national team titles.) Born in Kansas, Cliff had wrestled at Oklahoma A & M—he was never beaten in a wrestling match—and he'd played football at Kansas State (he was an All-American halfback). Cliff had once held the world record in the 50-yard low hurdles, too, and he'd received a doctorate from Kansas State in 1921—in veterinary medicine, although he'd never been a practicing veterinarian. Cliff Gallagher was also a certified referee. We frequently refereed tournaments together.

As a wrestling coach, Cliff was a little dangerous; he showed the Exeter boys a great number of holds that had been illegal for many years—the key-lock, the Japanese wrist-lock, various choke-holds and other holds that dated from a time when it had been legal to coax your opponent to his back by applying pain or the threat of asphyxiation instead of leverage. Ted explained to me that he always allowed Cliff to demonstrate these holds to the boys; at some point, following Cliff's demonstration, Ted would quietly take the time to tell the boys: "Not that one." The boys, of course, were eager to learn anything new, and Cliff had much to teach that *I'd* never seen before; some of Cliff's holds were new to Ted, too.

We had to be on our toes in the Exeter wrestling room that year. There would be some kid twisting another kid's head off, and Ted or I would jump in and break it up. We'd always ask, "Did Cliff show you that?"

"Yes, sir," the boy would say. "I think it's called a Bulgarian head-and-elbow." Whatever it was called, Ted or I would put a stop to it, but we would never have criticized Cliff for his efforts—Cliff was having a great time, and we adored him. So did the kids—I'm sure they were putting the Bulgarian head-and-elbow to good use, probably in their dormitories.

As a referee, Cliff was completely reliable. He had all the right instincts for when to stop a potentially dangerous situation, for how to anticipate an injury before it happened; he always knew where the edge of the mat was—and which wrestler was using it, to what advantage—and he never called stalling on the wrong wrestler (he always knew who was stalling). It was a mystery to me how Cliff had memorized the rule book; as a referee, he permitted not a single illegal hold. (As a coach, Cliff Gallagher taught every move and hold he knew—legal or not.) Cliff taught me to be much better as a referee than I'd ever been as a wrestler. Refereeing is *all* technique; unlike wrestling, refereeing doesn't call upon superior athletic ability—or expose the lack thereof.

I will always remember a maniacally mismanaged high-school tournament in Maine—Cliff and I were the only actual wrestlers among our fellow referees. In the preliminary rounds, Cliff and I were also the only referees who penalized a headlock without the arm contained—if you lock up a man's head, you're supposed to include one of his arms in the headlock. To encircle your opponent's head—*just* his head—is illegal. For the benefit of the assembled coaches *and* our fellow referees, Cliff put on a clinic between rounds; he made special emphasis of the headlock *with* an arm. This information was dismaying to the other referees, and to most of the coaches. One of them said, "It's too late in the season to be showin' 'em somethin' new."

"It's not new, it's *legal*," Cliff said.

"It's new, too," the guy said—I don't remember if he was a coach or a referee. In any case, he expressed the sentiment of the majority: they'd been using and accepting an illegal headlock all season—probably for years—and it was nothing but a nuisance to them to enforce the rule now.

"Johnny and I are calling the illegal headlock—is that clear enough?" Cliff told them. And so we did.

The points for a repeated illegal hold can mount against a wrestler quickly. Repeated violations lead to disqualification. In no time, Cliff and I were penalizing *and* disqualifying half the state of Maine. (We "disqualified" a few coaches who protested, too.) In the semifinals, I also disqualified a heavyweight for deliberately throwing his opponent on top of the scorer's table; I had twice warned and penalized this wrestler for continuing to wrestle off the mat—after the whistle blew. I'd even asked his coach if the heavyweight in question was *deaf.*

"No, he's just a little stupid," his coach replied.

When I disqualified the heavyweight, his parents came out of the stands and confronted me in the middle of the mat. I had no trouble recognizing who they were—they didn't have to introduce themselves. At a glance, I could see they'd swum forth from the same gene pool for enormity that had spawned their son. Cliff saved me.

"If you understand nothing else, you can understand one rule," Cliff told the heavyweight's parents. "It's just *one* rule and I'm only going to tell you *once.*" (I could see that he had their attention.) "This is a *mat,*" Cliff said, pointing to where we were standing. "And *that,*" Cliff said—pointing to the scorer's table where the heavyweight had thrown his opponent—"that is a goddamn table. In wrestling," Cliff said, "we do it on the *mat.* That's the rule." The heavyweight's parents shuffled away without a word. Cliff and I were alive until the finals.

The finals were at night. Scary people from the middle of Maine emerged in the night. (My good friend Stephen King doesn't make up *everything*; he knows the people I mean.) The fans for the finals that night made the disqualified heavyweight's parents seem mildly civilized. In rebellion over the illegal head-lock, our fellow referees had gone home; Cliff and I alternated refereeing the weight classes for the finals. When he was refereeing, I was the mat judge; Cliff was the mat judge when I was out on the mat refereeing. A mat judge can (but usually doesn't) overrule a referee's call; in a flurry of moves, sometimes the mat judge sees something the referee misses—for example, illegally locked hands in the top position—and in the area of determining the points scored (or not) on the edge of the mat, before the wrestlers are out of bounds, the mat judge can be especially effective.

There can be 11 or 12 or 13 weight classes in a high-school wrestling tournament. Nowadays, in the New England Class A tournament, the lightest weight class is 103 pounds—there are 13 weight classes, ending with the 189-pounder and the heavyweight (under 275). But in high schools there is occasionally a 100-pound class—in some states today there is also a 215- or 220-pound class, in addition to 189 and 275—and in Maine in '65 the heavyweight class was unlimited. (The weight class used to be *called* Unlimited.)

In the first three weight classes, Cliff and I gave out half a dozen penalty points for the illegal headlock—apparently a feature of Maine life—and Cliff bestowed one disqualification: for biting. Some guy was getting pinned in a crossface-cradle when he bit through the skin of his opponent's forearm. There was bedlam among the fans. What could possibly be more offensive to them than a no-biting rule? (There were people in the stands who looked like they bit other people every day.)

That night in Maine, Cliff Gallagher was 68. A former 145-pounder, he was no more than 10 pounds over his old weight class. He was pound-for-pound as strong as good old Caswell from Pitt. Cliff was mostly bald; he had a long, leathery face with remarkable ears—his neck and his hands were huge. And Cliff didn't like the way the crowd was reacting to his call. He went over to the scorer's table and took the microphone away from the announcer.

"No biting—is that clear enough?" Cliff said into the microphone. The fans didn't like it, but they quieted down.

We had a few more weight classes (and a lot more illegal headlocks) to get through; we kept alternating the matches, between referee and mat judge, and we kept blowing our whistles—in addition to the headlocks without an arm, there were over-scissors and full-nelsons and figure-four body-scissors and twisting knee-locks and head-butts, but there was no more biting. In the 177-pound class, I called the penalty that determined the outcome of the match; I thought the fans were going to rush me on the mat, and the coach of the penalized wrestler distinctly called me a "cocksucker"—normally another penalty, but I thought I'd better let it pass.

Cliff conferred with me while the crowd raged. Then he went to the microphone again. "No poking the other guy in his eyes over and over again—is that clear enough?" Cliff said.

It was Cliff who refereed the heavyweights, for which I was— for which I *am*—eternally grateful. The boy who'd been thrown on the scorer's table, and had thus been victorious in the semi-finals, was a little the worse for wear; his opponent was a finger bender, whom Cliff penalized twice in the first period—patiently explaining the rule both times. (If you grab your opponent's fingers, you must grab all four—not just two, or one, and not just his thumb.) But the finger bender was obdurate about finger bending, and the boy who'd been bounced off the scorer's table was already . . . well, understandably, *sensitive*. When his fingers were illegally bent, the boy responded with a head-butt; Cliff correctly penalized him, too. Therefore, the penalty points were equal as the second period started; so far, not one legal wrestling move or hold had been initiated by either wrestler—I knew Cliff had his hands full.

The finger bender was on the bottom; his opponent slapped a body-scissors and a full-nelson on him, which drew *another* penalty, and the finger bender applied an over-scissors to the scissors, which amounted to another penalty against *him*. Then the top wrestler, for no apparent reason, rabbit-punched the finger bender, and that was that—Cliff disqualified him for unsportsmanlike conduct. (Maybe I should have *let* him be thrown on the scorer's table without penalty, I thought.) Cliff was raising the finger bender's arm in victory when I spotted the losing heavyweight's mother; it was another easy gene-pool identification—this woman was without question a heavyweight's mom.

In Maine that year—*only* in Maine—I had heard us referees occasionally called "zebras." I presume this was a reference to our black-and-white-striped shirts, and I presume that Cliff had previously heard himself called a "zebra," too. Notwithstanding our familiarity with the slur, neither Cliff nor I was prepared for the particular assault of the heavyweight's mom. She lumbered manfully to the scorer's table and ripped the microphone from the announcer's hands. She pointed at Cliff, who was standing a little uncertainly in the middle of the mat when she spoke.

"Not even a zebra would fuck you," the mom said.

Despite the crowd's instinctive unruliness, they were as uncertain of how to respond to the claim made by the heavyweight's mother as Cliff Gallagher; the crowd stood or sat in stunned silence. Slowly, Cliff approached the microphone; Cliff may have been born in Kansas, but he was an old Oklahoma boy—he still walked like a cowboy, even in Maine.

"Is that clear enough?" Cliff asked the crowd.

It was a long way home from the middle of Maine, but all the way Cliff kept repeating, "Not even a zebra, Johnny." It would become his greeting for me, on the telephone, whenever he called.

That winter I took every refereeing job that I was offered. I didn't make much money, and I would never again see the likes of a tournament like that tournament in Maine. But the reason I was a referee at all, not to mention the reason I enjoyed it, was Cliff Gallagher. It was a great way to get back into wrestling.

"I told you—you're always going to love it," Ted Seabrooke said.

The Gold Medalist

In Iowa—I was a student at the Writers' Workshop from 1965 until 1967—Vance Bourjaily befriended me, but Vance was not my principal teacher. For a brief moment I tried working with Nelson Algren, who—except for the unnamed Instructor C– from my unsuccessful days in Pittsburgh—represented my first encounter with a critic of an *un*constructive nature. I was attracted to Mr. Algren's rough charm, but he didn't much care for me or my writing. I was "too fancy" a writer for his taste, he told me; and, worse (I suspect), I was not a city boy who'd been schooled on the mean streets. I was a small-town boy and a private-school brat; I was even more privileged than Algren knew—I was a "faculty brat." The best tutor for a young writer, in Mr. Algren's clearly expressed view, was real life, by which I think he meant an *urban* life. In any case, my life had not been "real" enough to suit him; and it troubled him that I was a wrestler, not a boxer—the latter was superior to the former, in Mr. A.'s opinion. He was always good-natured in his teasing of me, but there was a detectable disdain behind his humor. And I was not a poker player, which I think further revealed to Algren the shallowness of my courage.

My friend the poet Donald Justice (a very *good* poker player, I'm told) once confided to me that Mr. Algren lost a lot of money in Iowa City—coming down from Chicago, as he did, and expecting to find the town full of rubes. He took me for a rube—and certainly I *was*—but he caused me no lasting wounds. Creative Writing, if honest at all, must be an occasionally unwelcoming experience. I appreciated Mr. Algren's honesty; his abrasiveness couldn't keep me from liking him.

I would not see Nelson Algren again until shortly before his death, when he moved to Sag Harbor and Kurt Vonnegut brought him to my house in Sagaponack for dinner. Again I liked him, and again he teased me; he was good at it. This time he claimed not to remember me from our Iowa days, although I went out of my way to remind him of our conversations; admittedly, since they had been few and brief, it's possible that Algren *didn't* remember me. But in saying goodnight he pretended to confuse me with *Clifford* Irving, the perpetrator of that notorious Howard Hughes hoax; he appreciated a good scam, Mr. Algren said. And when Vonnegut explained to him that I was not *that* Irving, Algren winked at me—he was still teasing me. (You shouldn't take a Creative Writing course, much less entertain the notion of becoming a writer, if you can't take a little teasing—or even a lot.)

But, thankfully, there were other teachers at Iowa. I was tempted to study with José Donoso, for I admired his writing and found him gracious—in every way that Nelson Algren was not. Then, upon first sight, I developed a schoolboy's unspoken crush on Mr. Donoso's wife; thereafter I could never look him in the eyes, which would not have made for a successful student-teacher relationship. And so my principal teacher and mentor at the Iowa Writers' Workshop became Kurt Vonnegut. (I once had a brawl in a pool hall—convincingly demonstrating, although never to Nelson Algren and not in his presence, that wrestling is superior to boxing—because a fellow student at Iowa, a boxer, had called Mr. Vonnegut a "science-fiction hack"; this false charge was made without the offending student's having read a single one of Kurt's books, "only the covers.")

Did Kurt Vonnegut "teach" me how to write? Certainly not;

yet Mr. Vonnegut saved me time, and he encouraged me. He pointed out some bad habits in my early work (in my first novel-in-progress), and he also pointed out those areas of storytelling and characterization that were developing agreeably enough. I would doubtless have made these discoveries on my own, but later—maybe much later. And *time*, to young and old writers alike, is valuable.

Later, as a teacher—I taught at the Workshop from 1972 until 1975—I encountered many future writers among my students at Iowa. I didn't "teach" Ron Hansen or Stephen Wright or T. Cora-ghessan Boyle or Susan Taylor Chehak or Allan Gurganus or Gail Harper or Kent Haruf or Robert Chibka or Douglas Unger how to write, but I hope I may have encouraged them and saved them a little time. I did nothing more for them than Kurt Vonnegut did for me, but in my case Mr. Vonnegut—and Mr. Yount and Mr. Williams—did quite a lot.

I'm talking about technical blunders, the perpetration of sheer boredom, point-of-view problems, the different qualities of first-person and third-person voice, the deadening effect of expo-sition in dialogue, the crippling limitations of the present tense, the intrusions upon narrative momentum caused by puerile and pointless experimentation—and on and on. You just say: "You're good at that." And: "You're not very good at this." These areas of complaint are so basic that most talented young writers will even-tually spot their mistakes themselves, but perhaps at a time when a substantial revision of the manuscript might be necessary—or worse, after the book is published.

Tom Williams once told me that I had a habit of attributing mythological proportions and legendary status to my characters—he meant before my characters had *done* anything to earn such attribution. (The same could be said of García Márquez, but in my case Mr. Williams's criticism was valid.) And Kurt Vonnegut once asked me if I thought there was something intrinsically funny about the verbs "peek" and "peer." (What could be "intrinsically funny" about *verbs*? I thought. But Mr. Vonnegut meant that I overused these verbs to a point of self-conscious cuteness; he was right.)

When I was a student at the Iowa Writers' Workshop, Gail Godwin was a student there, and the future (1989) National Book Award winner John Casey was in my class—Gail and John were "taught" by Kurt Vonnegut, too.

Mr. Casey recently reminded me that Ms. Godwin was, upon her arrival in Iowa City, already a writer to take seriously. Casey recalled how Gail defended herself in the parking lot of the English & Philosophy Building from the unwanted attentions of a lecherous fellow student, who shall remain nameless.

"Please leave me alone," Ms. Godwin warned the offending student, "or I shall be forced to wound you with a weapon you can ill afford to be wounded by in a town this small."

The threat was most mysterious, not to mention writerly, but the oafish lecher was not easily deterred. "And what might that weapon be, little lady?" the lout allegedly asked.

"Gossip," Gail Godwin replied.

Andre Dubus and James Crumley were also students at the

Writers' Workshop then. I remember a picnic at Vance Bourjaily's farm, where a friendly pie-fight ensued; Dubus or Crumley, bare-chested and reasonably hairy, was struck in the chest by a Boston cream pie. Who threw the pie, and why, escapes my ever-failing memory—I swear I didn't do it. David Plimpton is a possible candidate. Plimpton and I were wrestling teammates at Exeter—he was the team captain a year ahead of me—and our being together in Iowa seemed an unlikely irony to us both. (Plimpton had wrestled at Yale.)

These were the days before the fabulous Carver-Hawkeye Arena; the Iowa wrestling room was up among the girders of the old fieldhouse. Dave McCuskey was the coach; he was friendly to me, but ever-critical of my physical condition. I was capable of wrestling, hard, with Coach McCuskey's boys, but only for three or four minutes; then I needed to sit down and rest on the mat with my back against the wrestling-room wall. McCuskey frowned upon this behavior: if I wasn't in shape to go head to head with his boys for "the full nine minutes," then I shouldn't be wrestling at all. I was content to shoot takedowns until I got tired; then I'd rest against the wall—and then I'd shoot a few more takedowns. Coach McCuskey didn't like me resting against the wall.

David Plimpton, who was as out-of-shape as I was, also enjoyed sparring with Coach McCuskey's Iowa wrestlers. Plimpton told me that McCuskey was similarly disapproving of him. From Plimpton's and my point of view, we were making a contribution: we were offering our aging bodies as extra workout partners for McCuskey's kids. But it was Coach McCuskey's wrestling room; he set the tone—and I respected him. No resting against the wall. As a consequence, my appearances (and Plimpton's) in the Iowa wrestling room were sporadic—I went there only when I wanted to punish myself.

A happy solution might have been for Plimpton and me to wrestle together, but Plimpton had been a 191-pounder at Yale (when I'd been a 130-pounder at Pitt); we'd both put on 15 or 20 pounds since then, but we couldn't wrestle together—there was about a 60-pound difference between us.

Seven years later, when I would go back to Iowa to teach at the Writers' Workshop, the wrestling room was still in the girders of the old fieldhouse but the atmosphere in the room had changed. Gary Kurdelmeir, a former national champion for Iowa in 1958, was the head coach. In '72, Kurdelmeir's new assistant coach arrived in Iowa City—Dan Gable, fresh from a Gold-Medal performance in the Munich Olympics at 149½ pounds. In Kurdelmeir and Gable's wrestling room, there were lots of "graduate students" (as Plimpton and I had been in 1965–67) and other postcollege wrestlers. The years I taught at the Workshop (1972–75) were the beginning of Iowa's dominance of collegiate wrestling under Dan Gable. (As the head coach, Gary Kurdlemeir won two national team titles for Iowa—in '75 and '76—but the head-coaching job would soon be Gable's; he won his first team championship in '78. J. Robinson, now the head coach at the University of Minnesota, became Gable's assistant.)

Brad Smith, Chuck Yagla, Dan Holm, Chris Campbell—they were all in the Iowa wrestling room at that time, and they would all become national champions. That wrestling room was the most intense wrestling room I have ever seen; yet Gable and Kurdlemeir were happy to have you there, contributing—even if you were good for no more than two minutes before you had to go rest against the wall. In that room, two minutes was all I was good for.

At several of Iowa's dual meets, I sat beside the former Iowa coach, Dave McCuskey, who was retired; as fellow spectators, Coach McCuskey and I had no philosophical differences of opinion. Everyone admired Gable: with three national collegiate titles at Iowa State (just *one* loss in his entire college career), he drew a crowd—not only at Iowa's matches but in the wrestling room. Everyone wanted to wrestle with him—if only for two minutes. In those years, I generally chose easier workout partners, but there were no easy workout partners in that Iowa room. Like everyone else, I couldn't resist the occasional thrill (and instant humiliation) of wrestling Dan Gable. I never scored a point on him, of course. In this failure, I was in good company: in the 1972 Olympics at Munich, where Gable won the Gold Medal, none of his opponents scored a point on him either.

To win the Olympics in freestyle wrestling without losing a single point is akin to winning the men's final at Wimbledon in straight sets, 6–0, 6–0, 6–0; or perhaps a four-game sweep of the World Series, while holding the losing team scoreless. It's rarer still that Gable's dominance as a wrestler has undergone the transition from competitor to coach with equal success: in 1995, Iowa won its fourth NCAA title of the last five years—and its fifteenth national championship of the last 21. In '95, Iowa also captured its 22nd straight Big 10 crown; I believe that's a record for consecutive collegiate championships—in any conference, in any sport. Out of 10 weight classes, the '95 Iowa team advanced seven wrestlers to the semifinal round of the NCAA tournament. Ever the perfectionist, Dan Gable was disappointed: Iowa's 150-pounder and 190-pounder were both defending national champions—in the finals, they both lost.

It's always the wrestling I remember; it marks the years. My memories of being a student at the Iowa Writers' Workshop, and of being a teacher there, frequently intermingle; I even confuse my fellow students with my students. But I can manage to sort out the years (not only in Iowa) by the workout partners that I had, and by recalling who the coach was—and in which wrestling room I worked out. And possibly it is a testimony to the practical, businesslike atmosphere of the Writers' Workshop that I remember my student days and my teaching days as much the same. I felt fortunate to be at Iowa—in both capacities.

The Death of a Friend

Don Hendrie, Jr., who was a classmate of mine at Exeter, although I hardly knew him there, was another student at the Iowa Workshop (in my *student* days); he is the author of four novels and one collection of short stories—in addition to serving for several years as the director of the graduate writing program at the University of

Alabama. The coincidence of my being at Iowa with Don Hendrie is an even more unlikely irony than my being there with David Plimpton, because, when Hendrie and I were students at Exeter, we both sought the affections of the same young woman; she married Hendrie, who in Iowa became my closest friend. Our children would grow up together. When I was teaching and coaching at a small college in Vermont, Hendrie would be teaching at a small college in New Hampshire—about an hour's distance. When he taught at Mount Holyoke College, I followed him there.

Hendrie had a habit of including the physical descriptions of his friends in his novels, where we would appear as characters under fictional names; this never offended me, because Hendrie's narrative voice was consistently teasing and affectionate. My last appearance in a Don Hendrie novel was as a character named Barry Kessler, a screenwriter, in *A Survey of the Atlantic Beaches*. He saw me as "a rabid, middle-aged athlete given to the long run and the heavy weight."

We had a lifelong argument about Oscar Wilde—Hendrie liked him, I don't. By the way, I bear no loathing for writers because they are minor; it isn't Wilde's being minor that troubles me. And my dislike of Wilde was never fueled by his homosexuality—that "gross indecency," as it was called in Britain at the time Wilde was sentenced to two years in prison, from which he never recovered. On the contrary, one has to like Oscar Wilde for championing "obscenity," as sodomy was then presumed to be. But what I hate about Wilde is that he was an inferior writer who delighted in aiming his one-liner wit at his superiors; did

he so envy Dickens and Flaubert that he felt compelled to scorn
them?

Wilde shouldn't have spent a day in jail for being "obscene,"
but posterity will relegate Wilde to where he belongs, which is
where he can already be most widely found: in coffee-table books
of harmless quotations. By comparison, Flaubert and Dickens
still have actual *readers*. (What is ordinary about Wilde is that
there's no shortage of writers whose lifestyles are more deserving
of attention than their work.)

I say all this because the centenary of Oscar Wilde's wrongful
imprisonment occurred as I was rewriting this memoir; predict-
ably, the centenary was not allowed to pass without all manner of
overpraise being heaped upon Wilde. Whereas I was prepared to
read that "Wilde's imprisonment ranks as one of literature's great-
est tragedies," I was *not* prepared to suffer the Wilde centenary
hyperbole in silence; yet my friend Don Hendrie had died—there
was no one else I wanted to argue about Oscar Wilde with.

Hendrie often found a means of furthering personal disputes
in his fiction, which I accepted as a charming eccentricity. "Barry
Kessler posed in the doorway with his hands on his hips," Hendrie
wrote. "He wore running shoes, fresh white socks to his knees,
filmy green shorts, and an immaculate T-shirt with the words
'Oscar Wilde Sucks' in diminutive letters over the breast pocket.
A short man, narrow of waist, large of chest, he had the gone-
craggy face of a former (and successful) child actor who had kept
his confidence and improved upon it with a great deal of strenu-
ous effort."

Don Hendrie died in March of '95, just two days before my son Colin's 30th birthday. Suffering from Parkinson's, Hendrie had lost his fine grasp of the language in a stroke four years earlier; his vocabulary had abandoned him. As a fellow writer, I admired how courageous and uncomplaining he was about losing his *words*. Only a month before he died, we were talking in my house in Vermont, and Hendrie—at a loss for the word he wanted—left the dinner table and walked into the kitchen. There he patiently patted the refrigerator. "*This* thing," he said, "where the food goes to be cold."

He had an automobile accident, in Maine, about a week or so later. When he was released from the hospital, he was frail and disoriented; in addition to the debilitation of the Parkinson's, something was wrong with his heart. He spent the night before he died at his ex-mother-in-law's house in Exeter with his elder son; they had breakfast together the next morning, and Hendrie died of a heart attack while walking around the block. He fell over on Front Street, the same street where I had grown up in my grandmother's house. (Hendrie wasn't a native of Exeter; he had attended the academy and married a town girl, but over the years Exeter had become a kind of home to him.)

It was Hendrie I sold my motorcycle to, when I became a father. We were married within a couple of years of each other; I was an usher at his wedding, in Exeter—the wedding reception was at the Exeter Inn, which is also on Front Street, where he died. (We were divorced within a couple of years of each other, too.)

I miss him. And when I think of him, I see him as a student

at Iowa when I was a student, too, and we would read aloud what we'd written to each other, and say things of small importance—such as, "Oscar Wilde sucks"—which, of course, were things we thought were of no small importance then.

I was newly married, and recently a father for the first time; Hendrie was in love, and about to be married—and soon to be a father, too. And, as writers—actually, would-be writers—we were just getting started. We both had jobs in the university library, restacking the returned books. We both had football-season jobs, selling pennants and buttons and stadium cushions and cowhorns and bells at the Iowa home games. We both worked as waiters in a nauseating restaurant out on the Coralville strip. The point is, Hendrie and I saw each other every day, and we were doing a variety of mindless things, but every day we were excited, because we were going to be writers. That's how I want to remember him.

What Vonnegut Said

I don't remember my fellow student Tom McHale, the future author of *Farragan's Retreat* and *Principato*. I must have met him in Iowa City, but I never really knew him, nor do I recall McHale's "terrific Belgian girlfriend"; the description is John Casey's—John has expressed his surprise that I fail to remember her. (Tom McHale died, an apparent suicide, in 1982; some say he had a heart attack.)

I do remember Jonathan Penner—tall and particularly striking-looking in profile. I recall him running laps on the indoor track, where I ran every day; in my memory, Penner was a strong and tireless runner—and a lot faster than I was. But my principal attentions at Iowa were given to my developing writing; in writers' memories, real people are often not as clear as our created characters. It wouldn't surprise me if Penner were to ring me up, upon reading this, and tell me that he never ran at all—not one lap. (It would amaze me, however, to hear that Jonathan Penner is a *short* person.)

Of course I could phone Andre Dubus and ask him if it was his chest or Crumley's that was splattered with Boston cream pie; I could call David Plimpton and ask him if he threw the pie, and whose chest he hit. But I believe the gaps and even the errors in my memory are truthfulness of another kind: what we fiction writers forget, or what we get wrong, is part of what a "memoir" means to us. (I do recall that Plimpton caused both envy and indignation by selling a short story to one of those magazines that are routinely concealed from wives and children, and that he spent the money on a shotgun, which prompted one sour fellow student to express the hope that Plimpton would use his new weapon on himself.)

And what of my classmates at Iowa who did *not* become writers? One of them is a high-school English teacher, and one of them is a law-school professor, and another one is a clinical psychologist. (The psychologist is David Plimpton.)

In addition to the many published writers among my students at Iowa, my two best students at Bread Loaf, Patty Dann and Elisabeth Hyde, and my best student at Brandeis, Carol Markson, are working novelists. But what about those Creative Writing students of mine—not only at Iowa but elsewhere—who did *not* go forth to take the literary world by storm? One of them is a highly respected editor in a venerable New York publishing house; another makes a rather good living writing Westerns; a third is the headmaster of a distinguished private school; many are English teachers, at both the high-school and the college level; and last but not least—in fact, this is someone I am particularly proud of—is a champion-class female bodybuilder, Karen Andes, who has written a book about strength conditioning for women. I was not of much help to Karen with her first novel, which remains unpublished, but I was the first person who took her to a gym and put a dumbbell in her hand. Now I am learning from her, for—at my age (I am 53)—a book about strength conditioning for female bodybuilders is considerably above my present capacities.

Yet what I remember best about being a student at Iowa was that sense of myself as being married, and being a father. It separated me from the majority of the other students; they had the time to talk about writing—my impression was that they talked about it endlessly. Except with Hendrie, I had no time for talking; I taught only one undergraduate writing course but I had three part-time jobs. When I wasn't working, I was either looking after my son Colin or I was writing.

We didn't have a television. When there was something of interest on TV, I put Colin in the stroller and walked around the block to the Vonneguts' house. It was in Kurt's house that I

The Phillips Exeter Academy wrestling team, 1961—Captain John Irving (front row, center). Irving's regular workout partners were Mike McClave (front row, second from right) and Al Keck (front row, second from left). Larry Palmer, who ate the famous half-pound piece of toast, is seated to Irving's right. The man in the coat and tie is Coach Ted Seabrooke. PHOTO: '61 PEAN

John Irving (on top) at 133 pounds in '61. Despite two undefeated dual-meet seasons, he never won a New England title. PHOTO: '61 PEAN

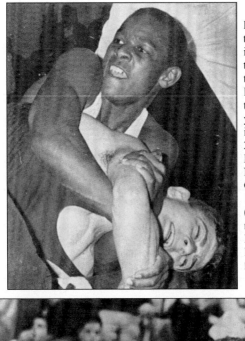

Larry Palmer (on top) at 121 pounds in '61—he failed to make weight at the New England Interscholastic tournament that year. In '62, six inches taller and 26 pounds heavier, Palmer won the New England Class A title at 147 pounds. (Larry Palmer is now Professor of Law at Cornell Law School.) PHOTO: '61 PEAN

Ted Seabrooke coaching 137-pounder Al Keck in '61. The fans are draped on the rails of the overhanging wooden track that circumscribed "the pit" at Exeter. PHOTO: '61 PEAN

Cliff Gallagher coaching in the Exeter wrestling room in 1966. It must be before practice, because the door to the wrestling room is partially open and there are so few bodies rolling around; Cliff always came to practice early. The boy sitting on the mat must be a first-year wrestler—he's not wearing wrestling shoes. PHOTO: BRADFORD F. HERZOG

In the University of Iowa wrestling room, 1973: Dan Gable catches John Irving with a foot-sweep.
PHOTO: GARY WINOGRAD

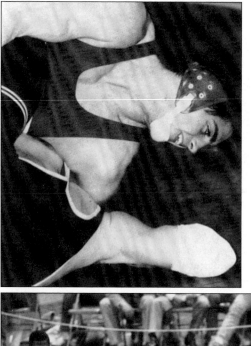

Irving's son Colin,
a 1983 prep-school
All-American
for Northfield
Mt. Hermon at
152 pounds—
Colin was also the
160-pound
New England
Class A Champion
in '83.

Colin Irving completing an upper-body throw in the '83 New
England Class A finals. Both the referee and the mat judge (upper
left) are anticipating the pin. Photo: C.F.N.I.

Colin driving his Exeter opponent's shoulders to the mat in the 160-pound finals. PHOTO: C.F.N.I.

A legal headlock: the head encircled with an arm contained—in this case, Colin has his opponent's head and *both* his arms contained. Colin's pin in the finals at 1:45 of the first period won him the Ted Seabrooke Memorial Trophy for the Outstanding Wrestler in the '83 New England Class A tournament. PHOTO: C.F.N.I.

Summer '84: brothers—Colin with Brendan in Bridgehampton, New York. Colin is 19, and at his heaviest—about 195 pounds. Brendan is 14; he weighs about 105 pounds.
PHOTO: MARY ELLEN MARK

Brendan Irving (right), a tall 135-pounder with a proneness to injury: knee surgery in '87; reinjured the knee in '88; in '89, a separated shoulder, a torn rotator cuff, a lost front tooth, two broken fingers (right hand), mononucleosis, and a championship title.
PHOTO: STEVE IRVING

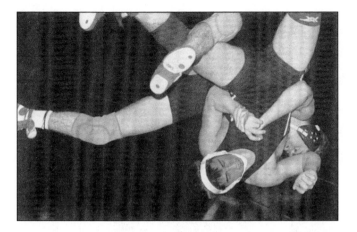

Brendan (black headgear) going for the pin: between 1984 and 1989, he won over 90 percent of his matches by a fall. Brendan was captain of the Vermont Academy team in '89. PHOTO: JANET IRVING

The semifinals: Brendan Irving, seeded fifth at 135 pounds, pins the number-one seed at 4:40 of the third period. Brendan pinned all his opponents in the '89 New England Class A tournament.
PHOTO: JANET IRVING

Coach Irving embracing son Brendan, seconds after Brendan won the '89 New England Class A title at 135 pounds—by a fall in 4:52 of the third period.

At 31 pounds, Everett looks like a future middleweight.

watched the Six-Day War, holding Colin on my lap. It was on the occasion of another television event, with Colin again on my lap or destroying some household possession of the Vonneguts', that I remember having a conversation with Kurt about what I would *do* to support my writing habit.

Teachers and coaches had been good to me, Kurt included. I presumed I would get a teaching job, and I would coach wrestling. I certainly had no illusions about my writing being self-supporting. I told Kurt that I wasn't going to make myself miserable by even imagining that I would make a living from my *writing*.

"You may be surprised," Vonnegut told me. "I think capitalism is going to treat you okay."

The Ph.D. Vote

My first teaching job was at Windham College (now defunct) in Putney, Vermont. Windham was one of those colleges that prospered, briefly, during the time of the Vietnam War; it was richly populated with students who wouldn't have been students if they hadn't been trying to stay out of Vietnam, but some of these non-students were the best Creative Writing students I ever had—and one real student among them was my future business manager, Willard Saperston. When the war was over, Windham folded, but by then I had already resigned.

There was no wrestling team at Windham when I came

there. I prevailed upon the college to buy a wrestling mat, which I installed in a former storage room of the fieldhouse, where I coached wrestling as a so-called club sport. About a half-dozen former high-school wrestlers, including a couple of Vietnam vets, were the core of the club; compared to every wrestling room I had ever worked out in, it was unsatisfactory, but I had my workout partners—I couldn't complain.

When the college went belly-up and auctioned all of its portable holdings, I went to the auction with the hope that I could buy the wrestling mat. But the mat was sold to a college down South as part of a package of athletic equipment—the whirlpool baths from the training room, and three sets of Universal Gyms, and all the free weights from the weight room. I don't think the buyer even wanted the mat—the college down South didn't offer wrestling as a sport— but I was unable to extricate the mat from the overall package.

Notwithstanding Windham's collapse, Putney was a good home for my children, and my primary residence for the 18 years of my first marriage; my ex-wife, Shyla, still lives there. The same Windham student who would become my business manager was also handy as a carpenter; on my Putney property, Willard Saperston converted a tool shed—one of the small outbuildings beside the barn—into an office for me. I would write the better part of five novels in that tiny box of a building, which Shyla has now restored to what it originally was: a tool shed. As I've said, Willard Saperston, who created my first office, now "manages" my money. (I sense a kind of symmetry to this story, not unlike my old friend

Don Hendrie dying within sight of the inn where he had his wedding reception and the house where I was born.)

And despite Windham's relatively short life, I would keep coming back to Putney. I went away for a year, to Vienna—where my second son, Brendan, was born in 1969—and I was three years away from Putney when I returned to Iowa to teach at the Workshop; there was another year away, when I first taught at Mount Holyoke; and another, when I taught at Brandeis. But in between those times away, I was in Putney, writing in the tool shed.

For the writing of my first four novels (*The World According to Garp* was my fourth) I usually had a full-time job—the two exceptions being an award from the Rockefeller Foundation (they don't give grants to individual writers anymore) and a Guggenheim Fellowship. I had only two years of being a full-time writer between 1967 and 1978; yet, in those 11 years, I wrote and published four novels.

There was one other year when I didn't teach Creative Writing or coach wrestling: that was when I took time off to write a screenplay of my first novel, *Setting Free the Bears*. In that year, I was never once paid at the agreed-upon time—I sent desperate telegrams from Vienna to Los Angeles, begging for the next installment of my screenwriting fee. Worse, I had no time for my day job, which was to write a second novel; and the screenplay, after five drafts, was never made into a film. The point being: this was less of a *writing* year than any year in which I taught and coached full-time.

A footnote: the fellowship I received from the National Endowment for the Arts, to complete my third novel, was not enough money for a family of four, which I was supporting, to live on for a single summer; I spent the "fellowship" to rebuild the only bathroom in the Putney house—and I took a summer job. I'm not complaining about having to get a job, *or* about the NEA—the NEA was only giving me what the NEA could afford.

I've heard many of my fellow writers say that a writer must make it on his own and not lean on the university for assistance; they say that a writer who teaches for his daily bread—so that he's not putting financial burdens on his writing—is not a real writer . . . only hedging his bets. But in my own experience I *wanted* my writing to be free from the pressure to publish it too soon—free from the need to make a living from it. Friends who were constantly interrupting their novels-in-progress to write for magazines, or who published novels badly in need of rewriting because they needed the advances, have suffered the constraints of time and money as, truly, I never did.

Nowadays, nothing angers me as much (from my fellow writers) as to see those fortunate souls who are self-supporting in the writing business make their insensitive pronouncements at various Creative Writing programs across the United States. In the presence of good writers who teach for a living, these best-selling authors are fond of denouncing the university as too-safe a haven; they frequently urge student writers to make it on their own—even, hypocritically, to starve a little. This is *idle* hypocrisy, of course; it is doubly hard to tolerate when the proselytizing author is expensively well-tailored and riding a multibook contract in 25 languages.

Creative Writing courses are an economic necessity for writers in this country; for the writers who teach them, they are essential to their lives *as writers*. And for those few students who truly benefit from them, they are a gift of encouragement and time; writers—young writers, particularly—need more of both.

There is a quandary here, however: not every writer can or should teach Creative Writing. Many of my writer friends are simply too standoffish for the requisite social contact of the job; some are preternaturally uncomfortable in the presence of "young people"—many more are too thin-skinned to endure the nastiness of English Department politics.

I once was a member of an English Department (at Windham) wherein a senior full professor proposed that any department member without a Ph.D. should not be permitted to vote on matters concerning the curriculum. I was the *only* member of that English Department without a Ph.D., and so I sought to defend myself by saying that I agreed; I even flattered my colleagues by telling them that the writing of a Ph.D. thesis was a "massive" accomplishment. I thought it fair to warn them, however, that I was soon going to publish my first novel, which they would surely accept as an undertaking equal to their theses; I would wait to have a vote in the department until my novel was published.

I felt it also fair to warn them that I intended to write a second novel, and a third—and, if I were able, many more after those— and that with the publication of each novel I expected to be granted an additional vote. To my surprise, my argument was not met with the good humor with which I had delivered my defense, but the proposition—that only Ph.D.s be permitted to vote on matters pertaining to the curriculum—was narrowly defeated.

Many writers I know would rather write nonstop for magazines or newspapers than subject themselves to the pompous lunacy of academics. But, in my case, I got up early to write—having children in the house helps. I met with my students in an organized fashion, I daydreamed through English Department meetings, and then I went to the wrestling room—to a great number and variety of wrestling rooms—and I forgot about everything for two hours. Fortunately for me, this meant I hurried my writing for no one. And I could turn a deaf ear to that contact with the university community which I know is truly odious and intolerable to many writers. The point being: writers *usually* need to support themselves by means other than that writing which they most desire to do. And the economics of being a writer aren't getting any better—except for the lucky few, like me.

My First Novel

In 1968 I was paid an advance of $7,500 for my first novel, which Random House published in 1969. Joe Fox was my editor. Still at Random House, and still my in-house editor there, Mr. Fox told me that the average advance for a literary first novel today—"with expectations similar to the expectations that I had for *Setting Free the Bears*"—is $12,500. (Richard Seaver, my editor at Arcade, disputes Mr. Fox's figures; Mr. Seaver argues that the more common figure today is *still* $7,500.)

In 1968, with a wife and one child, I could *almost* have lived for a year on $7,500, but the pressures this would have put on me to too-hastily produce a second novel were unwelcome. I kept my teaching and coaching jobs, and I wrote my second novel—and my third and fourth—at a restrained pace.

Trust me: it was more possible for a family of three to live on $7,500 in 1968 than it is even imaginable for a family of three to survive on $12,500 today—for the moment assuming that Joe Fox's higher figure for an "average advance" is correct. And what did *Setting Free the Bears* actually sell? About 8,000 hardcover copies—a good number for that time, far exceeding both my publisher's and my own expectations. A first printing of a novel of a similar kind, today, would run between 7,500 and 10,000 copies—with the notable difference that, *today*, a sale of 8,000 copies would make neither the publisher nor the author feel at all as secure as Joe Fox and I were made to feel in 1969.

(I never expected, not quite 10 years later, that *The World According to Garp* would enable me to support myself by my writing alone. I don't miss teaching Creative Writing—it was hard and time-consuming work. But it was honorable, worthwhile work, and of use to my students—if only to a few of them.)

In a separate conversation I asked Mr. Fox if he would publish *Setting Free the Bears* if it came across his desk at Random House

today. My friend Joe hesitated, just a moment too long, before saying, "Well, yes, *but* . . ." I think the answer is no.

My Two Champions

I taught Creative Writing, at one place or another, for a total of
11 years; yet I continued to coach wrestling long after the publication of *The World According to Garp* freed me of the financial need
for an outside job. I coached until 1989, when I was 47, not only
because I preferred coaching to teaching but for a variety of other
reasons; the foremost reason was the success of my two elder sons
in the sport—they were better wrestlers (and better athletes) than
I had been, and coaching them meant more to me than my own
modest accomplishments as a competitor.

Colin, who wrestled at Northfield Mount Hermon, was a
prep-school All-American at 152 pounds—at the annual Lehigh
tournament in 1983. Colin also won the New England Class A
title at 160 pounds in '83; ironically, he pinned a guy from Exeter
in the finals. Colin was voted the Outstanding Wrestler in the
Class A tournament, for which he received the Ted Seabrooke
Memorial trophy. I would have been happier if Ted had been alive
to see Colin win the championship. Ted had seen Colin wrestle
only once, when Colin was just starting the sport.

"He's got much longer arms than *you* ever had," Coach
Seabrooke told me. "You ought to show him a crossface-cradle."

By the time Colin was a Class A Champion and an All-American, he was pinning half his opponents with a crossface-cradle.

At six feet two and a half, Colin was tall for a middleweight. I think that his college coach was well intentioned but mistaken to put Colin on a weight-lifting program in order to beef him up to the 177-pound class, and then to 190. Colin was not a natural light heavyweight; he was at his best as a *tall* middleweight. Nowadays—Colin is 30 years old—he stays out of the weight room and rides a mountain bike; he's a very lean 175.

His younger brother Brendan was, like me, a lightweight; *un*like me, Brendan was a *tall* lightweight—at five feet eleven and a half, Brendan is so thin that he looks like a six-footer. (I'm only five feet eight, "normal" for a lightweight.) Unremarkably, both Colin and Brendan grew up in wrestling rooms; rolling around on a mat was second nature to them—I remember that Brendan learned to walk on a wrestling mat. Unlike Colin, who didn't start competing as a wrestler before his prep-school years, Brendan had already won six junior-school New England tournaments before his prep-school career began. (Brendan won his first wrestling tournament at the weight of 82½ pounds.) By the time Brendan was wrestling for Vermont Academy, the other wrestlers—and, especially, the other coaches—in the New England Class A league were watching him closely to see if he would live up to the reputation of being Colin Irving's little brother; this was a burden for Brendan, largely because his proneness to injury was unlike anything Colin had ever suffered.

Brendan placed third in the New England Class A tournament

his sophomore year at Vermont Academy; it was a good finish to a bad season for him, because the tournament was only a month after he'd had knee surgery for torn cartilage—he'd missed most of the '87 season. In '88, he was seeded second in the Class A tournament; he'd had an undefeated dual-meet season, excepting two losses to injury-default. Then, in the semifinals of the tournament, he reinjured the knee and was pinned by a boy he'd pinned earlier in the season; the injury forced him to drop out of the Class A's—and he reinjured the same knee at the Navy wrestling camp in Annapolis that summer. He spent the rest of the summer and the fall in physical therapy.

Colin lost a close match in the Class A finals his junior year—to a boy he'd beaten easily in the dual-meet season. Colin didn't win the New England Class A title until his senior year. Brendan's senior year began badly. A separated shoulder and a torn rotator-cuff tendon eliminated him from a Christmas tournament. Brendan was the 1989 team captain at Vermont Academy, but he would spend the heart of the season on the bench. When his shoulder healed, he was back in the lineup for three matches; he won all three—then he sat out another three weeks with mononucleosis. (Then he knocked out a front tooth.)

The week before the New England Class A's, Brendan was wrestling at St. Paul's when the St. Paul's wrestler, who was losing at the time and repeatedly being put in a crossface-cradle, bent back two of Brendan's fingers on his right hand and broke them at the big knuckle joints. Under the finger-bending rule (all four or none), Brendan won the match, despite having to default with the injury. But the damage had been done: the fingers wouldn't heal by the time of the tournament—Brendan would wrestle at the Class A's with two broken fingers.

To add insult to injury, the mother of the St. Paul's wrestler objected to the referee's decision to award the match to Brendan because of her son's illegal hold; when a wrestler is injured by an illegal hold, and cannot continue wrestling, he wins. But the St. Paul's mother declared that Brendan had been injured prior to the match; she'd seen a Band-Aid on one of his fingers—one of the now-broken fingers. (Brendan had skinned a knuckle while scraping the ice off his car's windshield that morning, on his way to weigh in.) I had to restrain myself from sending the St. Paul's mother a videocassette of the match. The St. Paul's wrestler not only clearly broke Brendan's fingers; with his other hand, Brendan was pointing to his bent fingers—to draw the referee's attention to the foul—when the two fingers broke. The ref had made the right call, but he should have spotted the injury-in-progress—he could have prevented it.

Given the accumulation of Brendan's injuries, and his small number of matches in the '89 season, the seeding committee at the New England Class A tournament was entirely justified in seeding Brendan no higher than fifth in the 135-pound class; there were seven other wrestlers in the weight class with winning records. As his coach—I was an assistant coach at Vermont Academy for one year and the head coach for Brendan's last two seasons—I had contemplated moving Brendan up to the 140-pound class. In previous seasons, Brendan had pinned the two best wrestlers who would be the finalists in that weight class; in the 1989 Class A's, 140 was a weaker weight than 135. But Brendan, who was always admirably stubborn—even as a small child—insisted that 135 was *his* weight class; he didn't want to move up. (No wrestler wants to move *up* a weight class.)

The New England Class A tournament was at Exeter that year—in the new gym, where I'd never wrestled. (I have no idea what the pit is used for now.) I had a good team at little Vermont Academy in '89. In the Class A team standings, we would finish third—behind Deerfield and Exeter, two much bigger schools. I would send three Vermont Academy wrestlers to the finals, and two of them would win—Brendan was one of Vermont's two champions. He pinned the number-four seed from Northfield Mount Hermon in the quarterfinals, he pinned the number-one seed from Hyde in the semifinals, and he pinned the number-two seed from Worcester in the finals; he stuck his broken fingers, which were rebroken in the semifinals, in a bucket of ice between the rounds.

Tom Williams, who would die of cancer in three years, came to the tournament. Colin was there. My wife, Janet, was there; for two years, she'd not missed a match of Brendan's—and she'd taken what seemed, at the time, to be an excessive number of photographs. (As time passes, I'm grateful for every picture.) My mother had come up from Florida to see the tournament. And my old Exeter teammate, Charles C. ("Brute") Krulak—*General* Krulak—had come to see Brendan, too. Chuck had seen Brendan win the Lakes Region tournament (now known as the Northern New England tournament) the previous year; he'd promised Brendan that he would come to see him wrestle in the New England Class A's—but only if Brendan would promise to win the tournament. Brendan had promised, and Brendan had done it. (To be truthful, I'd always known he *could*. But he'd been so banged-up, I didn't think he *would*.)

I had spent so many hours of my life at wrestling tournaments, and so many more hours in wrestling rooms. After Exeter and Pittsburgh and Iowa and Windham, there were the hours in the wrestling room at Amherst College and at the Buckingham Browne & Nichols School—and at Harvard, at the New York Athletic Club, at Northfield Mount Hermon, and at Vermont Academy, too. It was the perfect closure . . . that it should end at Exeter, where it began. I knew I would still be a visitor to the occasional wrestling room, and that I would still put on the shoes—if only to roll around on the mat with Colin or Brendan, or with another old *ex*-wrestler of my generation—but my life in wrestling effectively ended there.

I put my Vermont Academy wrestlers on the team bus with my co-coach, Mike Kennelly, and I asked Mike and the team to forgive me for not riding on the bus with them one last time. I wanted to ride back to Vermont in Colin's car, with Colin and Brendan. On the long drive home (we were still somewhere in New Hampshire), Colin picked up a speeding ticket—shortly after delivering a lecture to Brendan and me about the infallibility of his new radar-detection system. But we could laugh about the ticket. Brendan, like his brother before him, had won the New England Class A title. It was the happiest night of my life.

My Last Weigh-in

I suppose I could mope around, wishing that my wrestling career, as a competitor, had ended half as happily as my life as a coach. But I think I've been lucky: I've always taken more pleasure from my children than I have from myself; I enjoy my children, and I try not to drive them—I drive myself.

In 1976, I was in the middle of *The World According to Garp*, and I was struggling with it—the novel had three first chapters, and I couldn't decide whether Garp or his mother was the main character. I had applied for a Guggenheim, but I didn't know that this time I was going to get one—I'd applied and *hadn't* gotten one before. I was teaching at Mount Holyoke—an all-women's college in South Hadley, Massachusetts—and I was working out in the wrestling room at Amherst College.

Henry Littlefield was the coach at Amherst then; Henry was a heavyweight—everything about him was grand. He was more than expansive, he was eloquent; he was better than good-humored, he was jolly. Henry was very rare, a kind of Renaissance man among wrestling coaches, and the atmosphere in the Amherst wrestling room was, to Henry's credit, both aggressive and good-natured—a difficult combination to achieve.

I was living in a faculty house on the edge of the Mount Holyoke athletic fields—Colin and Brendan had a great "yard" to play in, and the college pool to swim in. I arranged my classes so that I could run or use the weight room at the Mount Holyoke gym in the early morning; I would write for a couple of hours at midday—and again, late at night, after the children were in bed. In the afternoons, I would drive to the Amherst wrestling room; I often took Colin with me—he was 10 and 11 that wrestling season.

I weighed 162 when that season began; there was a postseason open tournament at Springfield College, and I intended to enter it at 136½ pounds. I was 34; the weight came off a little harder than it once had. After three months, I was holding my weight pretty easily at 142; the rest, as wrestlers frequently say, was "just water." That was all I was drinking in those months— just water. I had half a grapefruit with a teaspoon of honey for breakfast, and usually an apple or a banana; I had a bowl of oatmeal with a teaspoon of maple syrup for lunch; for dinner, I had some steamed fish and vegetables—lots of vegetables.

The last week before the tournament I was consistently weighing under 140, but I couldn't get under 138—that was the "water." Then I got sick; I had bronchitis, and the antibiotic was intolerable on my empty stomach. The doctor told me I had to eat to save my stomach, or give up the antibiotic; I couldn't give up the antibiotic because I couldn't wrestle with bronchitis. I tried to soothe my stomach with a little yogurt, or some skim milk. I felt better, but in two days I weighed 145. I couldn't make the 136½-pound class, although I knew it was my best wrestling weight. The next weight class was 149½; I started eating more oatmeal, and I added some rice to the steamed fish and vegetables.

At Springfield I weighed in at 147, with all my clothes on—and I'd eaten breakfast before the weigh-ins. The other contenders at 149½ were stripped naked; they exhaled their last breath before stepping on the scales. I tried not to notice how big they were. I was in the training room, getting taped—I had had a "loose" left pinky finger all season; it kept dislocating at the big knuckle joint—and Colin was looking grim. He was just beginning to get interested in wrestling; he had watched every detail of the weigh-ins.

"What are you thinking, Colin?" I asked him.

"You look like a thirty-six-pounder, Dad," Colin said.

I had never thought of the tournament at Springfield as my last tournament; all I'd hoped was to win one or two matches— and maybe place. It hadn't occurred to me that *watching* me lose might be painful for Colin. For Brendan, who was only six that spring, watching me wrestle, win or lose, was no big deal. Colin was old enough to realize that losing a wrestling match took a lot more out of me than losing a couple of sets of weekend tennis to a friend.

I drew a wild man in the first round. "Talent is overrated," Ted Seabrooke used to say. The guy was talented, and very dangerous, but he was also stupid. I was overcautious in the first period; I pulled out of a couple of sure takedowns because I was afraid of an upper-body throw that the wild man appeared to like in the underhook position—I came out ahead on takedowns, anyway. It was in the top position that the wild man was most dangerous. He was a leg man, and he hit me with a cheap tilt off a cross-body ride. (I was lucky it was only the tilt I got caught in; what the leg man was looking for was a bent-leg Turk—very uncomfortable.) I'd been leading 6–3, but the near-fall tied it up at 6–6—and I was still on the bottom. Off the whistle, the leg man put in his near leg for the cross-body ride again, but this time I drilled his head into the mat before he could tie up my far arm; it was a most basic defense against a cross-body ride. Ted Seabrooke had warned me that the move wouldn't work against a *good* leg man, but this guy wasn't good—he was sloppy.

At first I thought I'd given him a concussion, but the wild man needed only 45 seconds of injury time to clear his head. He was angry at me. It's stupid to be angry at your opponent when you wrestle; also, my move had been perfectly legal—it was a Ted Seabrooke move, not a Cliff Gallagher move.

The referee had blown the whistle for the injury without giving me points for my reversal, so the score was still 6–6—and I was still on the bottom. Off the whistle, Talented-but-Stupid put in his near leg again; once again, I protected my far arm and drilled his head into the mat. This time, the wild man needed a full minute to clear his head; thus he ran out of injury time—I won by injury default. The leg man was still angry; I could tell he thought he would have won the match if only I hadn't kept banging his head into the mat. I tend to think that he would have won, too; he seemed tireless to me—Tireless-but-Stupid. The wild man told me he hoped he would see me in one of the consolation rounds. If I lost in one of the championship rounds, at any time before the finals, I would drop down to the wrestle-backs, to the consolation brackets. It was conceivable that, if the leg man kept winning consolation matches, we would meet again. I hoped not.

("There is no such thing as *half* a cross-body ride," Coach Seabrooke used to say. "If you put a leg in, you've got to get hold of something else—unless you *want* to get your head drilled into the mat.")

In the locker room, the wild man with the headache was slamming lockers and kicking benches. I tried to stay away from him, but he followed me into the training room, where I had to have my "loose" left pinky finger retaped.

"I don't like anybody fuckin' with my head!" the leg man told me.

I felt old—I felt like a coach, not like a wrestler. Quoting Ted Seabrooke, I said: "If you put a leg in, you've got to get hold of something else—unless you *want* to get your head drilled into the mat."

"Shit!" the wild man shouted. (An inexplicable utterance—on a level of intelligence with *half* a cross-body ride.)

I was glad that Colin was in the stands with Brendan. Don Hendrie was in the stands with his children, too. When I was retaped, I went back up on the floor of the gym where the mats were laid out. A couple of Amherst wrestlers were also entered in the tournament; I watched their matches—all day, we would take turns coaching each other.

The toughest-looking kid in my weight class was a guy from the Coast Guard Academy; he was very slick on his feet, and he liked the high-crotch series for takedowns—my best defense, my whizzer, was worthless against a high-crotch. I knew I would have trouble with the guy from the Coast Guard, but I made the mistake of looking ahead, in the brackets, to my match with him; I overlooked the guy I had to wrestle in the next round.

He was someone in the military. He told me later he'd been stationed in Germany and had wrestled a lot of Greco-Roman matches over there; at the time, I think, he was stationed somewhere in New Jersey. I had my mind on the guy from the Coast Guard Academy, an error in concentration—and further indication, to me, that it was time to be a coach and not a wrestler. I gave up a couple of avoidable takedowns in the first period. Trailing by only three points in the second, I panicked too early and took an out-of-position shot at a takedown; he countered me to my back. When I fought off my back, I was trailing by seven points. Now it was time to panic. I managed an escape before the end of the period, but I couldn't complete a takedown before the buzzer; starting the third, I was six points behind. I got another escape, and a takedown, and he was hit with a penalty point for stalling; I rode him out, in the final period (I picked up another point for riding time), but I was aware of myself as a 36-pounder trying to turn a 49-pounder—he was too big to turn. I lost by a point. It was a respectable match, but I'd given it away in the first period. "Mental mistakes," Coach Seabrooke would have told me.

I dropped down into the consolation brackets and was pinned in my first match. I had scored with a snap-down in the first period—I was leading 2–1, because the guy had escaped from me following my takedown, when I got caught in a nice upper-body move: a bear hug with an inside trip. I was pinned before I could get my breath back. When I went to the training room, to get untaped, I saw that my left pinky finger was pointing straight up from the back of my hand; it was dislocated at the big knuckle joint again, but I was unaware of when or how it had happened. The trainer popped the finger back in place.

I was sitting on the training table, with my left hand packed in ice, when my opponent from the second round—the guy who'd been stationed in Germany and who was still in the military in New Jersey—came into the training room to ice his neck. He'd run into the guy from the Coast Guard Academy in the semi-finals—he'd lost—and he wanted to know about the guy who'd just pinned me; he was a boy from Springfield College. I told the military man to watch out for the bear hug with the inside trip.

I still wasn't thinking that this was my last tournament; I didn't feel bad, although I was angry at myself for getting pinned. Then the military man and I shook hands, and I wished him luck the rest of the way; since I'd been eliminated from the tournament, and my children were there, I thought it was time to take the children home. I felt like having a beer, and eating as much as my shrunken stomach would hold.

In parting, the military man said: "Nice match, sir."

That was all. That was it. He meant me no harm. But the damage was done. He was probably 24, and I was 34, but when he called me "sir," I felt older than I feel now, at 53; I felt ancient. It was time to be a coach, but not a wrestler.

Later, I phoned Ted Seabrooke. (At the time, Ted's death was four years away; he'd been sick, but I had no idea how bad things were going to get for him—I doubt that he knew either.) I gave Ted the results of the tournament, and I told him that I'd decided to call an end to competing as a wrestler—I told him the "sir" story.

"Johnny, Johnny," Coach Seabrooke said. "If the guy's in the military, he calls *everyone* 'sir.'" Incredibly, that hadn't occurred to me. But the damage had been done.

It was the last time I would weigh in. Only a week before the tournament, I'd weighed 138 pounds. At the tournament, I'd weighed 147—in all my clothes. When I weighed myself after Easter dinner, that same spring of '76, I weighed 165 pounds—my "natural" weight. (I weigh 167 pounds today.)

I remember that, 12 days after Brendan won the Class A title at 135 pounds, we were in a gym in Anguilla in the British West Indies. I was riding the stationary bike and Brendan was fooling around with the treadmill, making it go as fast as it could—and then trying to jump on it, and stay on it, while it was running. There were scales in the locker room; before we went for a swim, Brendan stripped down and weighed himself. Only 12 days earlier, I had seen him weigh in at 134½ pounds—now he weighed 152. That was six years ago. It was only yesterday that I called Brendan in Colorado.

"What do you weigh?" I asked him. (Wrestlers always ask this question.)

There was a pause while Brendan left the phone to weigh himself, and I overheard the O. J. Simpson trial on CNN—all the way from Colorado. (I was phoning from Vermont.) Then Brendan came back to the phone.

"One-fifty-two," he told me.

(As of this writing, my third son, Everett, who was born in Rutland, Vermont, in October of '91, is three and a half years old; he weighs 31 pounds. It is my observation that Everett is tall for his age, and his weight is slightly below average for his height. His hands look large, compared to the rest of him. If I had to hazard a guess, I'd say he looks like a future middleweight.)

Merely a Human Being

My involvement with wrestling has been widely misunderstood, even among my friends. John Cheever was a friend to me when we both taught at Iowa; he was a fan of Italian cooking, as I am, and we used to watch Monday Night Football at my house in Iowa City over a dish of pasta. Cheever once wrote a letter to Allan Gurganus in which he said: "John has always struck me as having been saddened by the discovery that to have been captain of the Exeter wrestling team was a fleeting honor."

Mr. Cheever was terribly correct, and often right about many things: he once warned me that it was a weakness in my writing that I described sexual acts and people consuming food, for these things were best enjoyed when not described; yet he mistook whatever had "saddened" me for the wrestling, the honors of which were never "fleeting" to me. Long after I stopped competing—and after I stopped coaching, too—the discipline remained. (My life in wrestling was one-eighth talent and seven-eighths discipline. I believe that my life as a writer consists of one-eighth talent and seven-eighths discipline, too.)

Nor am I inclined to complain about my wrestling-related surgeries—both knees, my right elbow, my left shoulder. Of the four operations, only the shoulder was major; a detached rotator-cuff tendon is no fun. But even the injuries that led to these surgeries are of lasting (not "fleeting") honor to me. My first knee (torn cartilage) was injured when I was fooling around with J. Robinson in the workout room at the Meadowlands Arena, during a break between sessions at the 1984 NCAA tournament; my other knee was hyperextended when I was wrestling with one of Brendan's teammates at Vermont Academy in '88—a good kid named Joe Black. (Joe was a three-time New England Class A Champion at 160 and 171 pounds.) Sometime between the knee injuries, my elbow was hyperextended at the New York Athletic Club—I was working out with Colin. And my shoulder succumbed, more gradually, to an accumulation of separations and rotator-cuff tears; what finally detached the supraspinatus tendon from the humerus wasn't a wrestling injury at all—rather, I fell off a children's slide with Everett in my arms (he was two), and in an effort to cover him up, and not land on him, I landed on my bad shoulder. Everett, who landed on my chest, was fine. (Had Coach Seabrooke been present to observe the fall, he would have reminded me that my standing side-roll had always been better executed to the right than to the left.)

I have no doubt that I have learned more from wrestling than from Creative Writing classes; good writing means *re*writing, and good wrestling is a matter of re*doing*—repetition without cease is obligatory, until the moves become second nature. I have never thought of myself as a "born" writer—any more than I think of myself as a "natural" athlete, or even a good one. What I am is a good *re*writer; I never get anything right the first time—I just know how to revise, and revise.

And for me to continue coaching wrestling, when there was no longer any financial need, was not a strain; coaching was never as time-consuming as teaching. At the prep-school level, where I chiefly coached, wrestling is a seasonal sport; and neither my presence in the gym nor the hours riding on the team bus took anything away from that part of me that was a writer—on the contrary, wrestling was an escape from writing; it was a release— whereas *talking* about writing, as one must to "teach" it, exercised many of the same muscles I needed for my own work.

Another factor, the videocassette recorder, has entered the world of coaching—the coaching of *any* sport. To my knowledge, there is no such handy tool available for Creative Writing classes. For example: my 189-pounder walks dejectedly off the mat, once more a loser, and once again because every time he stands up to escape from the bottom position his elbows are flailing a foot away from his rib cage—therefore, he is easily tight-waisted and thrown to his face. When I would invariably point out to him that even an object as large as his head could have passed through the space left between his elbows and his ribs (during his feeble standup attempt), he would say, "My elbows were tight to my sides, Coach—he just *did* something to them!"

But then would come the next day's film session, where, in front of his snickering teammates, I would show my 189-pounder the footage of his pathetic standup (with his elbows flapping as far from his body as a chicken's clipped wings in mock flight). I would slow-motion it, I would rewind it and slow-motion it again; in later years I could freeze-frame it, too—and that would be the end of arguing with him (until, naturally, he did it again). But I had a backup: the camera made my criticism valid.

There is no such indisputable backup in Creative Writing classes; frequently the student who perpetrates the deeply flawed story is adored and supported by his or her peers. A teacher's triumphs are few. You say: "When the father drops dead with an apple in his mouth while urinating on the front fender of his mother-in-law's car . . . uh, well, I just had trouble *seeing* it." Whereupon the student breaks into tears and confesses that this actually happened to her own father, in exactly the way she described it; and there then must follow, always unsatisfactorily, the timeless explanation that "real life" must be made to *seem* real—it is not believable solely for the fact that it *happened*. The truth is, the imagination can select more plausible details than those incredible-but-true details that we remember.

This is a tough sell to students rooted in social realism, and young writers without the imagination to move beyond autobiographical fiction—namely, to that host of first novelists who treat a novel as nothing but a thinly masked rendition of their lives up to that point.

Nor are the earliest efforts young writers make to *escape* auto-biographical fiction necessarily successful. A student of mine at Iowa—a brilliant fellow, academically; he would go on to earn a Ph.D. in something I can't even pronounce or spell—wrote an accomplished, lucid short story about a dinner party from the point of view of the hostess's fork.

If you think this sounds fascinating, my case is already lost. Indeed, the young writer's fellow students worshiped this story and the young genius who wrote it; they regarded my all-too-apparent indifference to the fork story as an insult not only to the author but to all of them. Ah, to *almost* all of them, for I was saved by a most unlikely and usually most silent member of the class. He was an Indian from Kerala, a devout Christian, and his accent and word order caused him to be treated dismissively—as someone who was struggling with English as a second language, although this was not the case. English was his first language, and he spoke and wrote it very well; the unfamiliarity of his accent and the cadence, even of his written sentences, made the other students regard him lightly.

Into the sea of approval that the fork story was receiving, and while my "but . . ." was repeatedly drowned out by the boisterous air of celebration in the class, the Indian Christian from Kerala said, "Excuse me, but perhaps I would have been moved if I were a fork. Unfortunately, I am merely a human being."

That day, and perhaps forever after, *he* should have been the teacher and I should have given my complete attention to him. He is not a writer these days, except on the faithful Christmas cards he sends from India, where he is a doctor. Under the usual holiday greetings, and the annual photograph of his increasing family, he writes in a firm, readable hand: "Still merely a human being."

On my Christmas cards to him, I write: "Not yet a fork."

(I used to say this to my students in Creative Writing: the wonderful and terrifying thing about the first page of paper that awaits the first sentence of your next book is that this clean piece of paper is completely unimpressed by your reputation, or lack thereof; that blank page has not read your previous work—it is neither comparing you to its favorite among your earlier novels nor is it sneering in memory of your past failures. That is the absolutely exhilarating and totally frightening thing about beginning—I mean each and every new beginning. That is when even the most experienced teacher becomes a student again and again.)

And what about the fork author—where is he today? In Boston, I believe; more pertinent, he's a published novelist—and a good one. I much admired his first novel, and was overall relieved to see that the characters in it were human beings—no cutlery among them.

Alas, these generally pleasant memories should not conceal the fact that I must have played the Nelson Algren role to more than one of my writing students. I'm certain that I've hurt the feelings of young writers who were more serious and gifted than I judged them to be. But just as Mr. Algren didn't harm me by his blunt and (I think) unfair assessment, I doubt that I have harmed any *real* writers; real writers, after all, had better get used to being misunderstood.

When it happens to me, I just remind myself of what Ted Seabrooke told me: "That you're not very talented needn't be the end of it."

AUTHOR'S NOTES

A few pages of this memoir were written as a letter to John Baker, Editorial Director at *Publishers Weekly;* John published parts of my letter to him in an article he wrote for *PW* (June 5, 1995). Portions of my remembrance of Don Hendrie were published in the form of an obituary for Hendrie that I wrote for *The Exeter Bulletin* (Fall 1995). And an excerpt from "The Imaginary Girlfriend" appeared in a fall '95 issue of *The New Yorker.*

I am grateful to Deborah Garrison at *The New Yorker* and to my wife, Janet, for their editorial response to an earlier draft of this autobiography, which was called "Mentors" and (believe it or not) contained fewer than 10 pages about wrestling. Deb and Janet ganged up on me; they said, in effect, "Are you kidding? Where's the wrestling?"

The reason this memoir was written at all is because I had shoulder surgery a week before Christmas, 1994. I was completely unprepared for how many hours a day, and for how many months, I would be rehabilitating my shoulder; I had anticipated an easier recovery. I knew there would be a little bone sawing in the area of the acromion-clavical joint, and I knew I had a torn rotator-cuff tendon; I *didn't* know that the tendon was detached from the humerus—nor did the surgeon, until he got in there.

With four hours of physical therapy a day, for four months, I didn't feel the time was right for me to begin a new novel, which I'd planned to begin after Christmas; I had about 200 pages of notes for the novel, and a halfway-decent first sentence, but the shoulder rehabilitation was too distracting.

One day in January of '95 I was making a nuisance of myself in my wife's office; I was aimlessly bothering Janet and her assistant—poking my nose into the pile of manuscripts that are always waiting to be read in the office of a literary agent. The stitches had only recently been removed from my shoulder, and I had just begun the requisite physical therapy; I was still wearing a sling, and I was bored.

Janet doesn't like it when I hang around her office. "Why don't you get out of here?" she said. "Go write a novel."

Summoning my most self-pitying voice, I said, "I can't write a novel with one arm and four hours a day of rehabilitation."

"Then go write a memoir, or something," Janet said. "Just get out of here."

My goal was to write an autobiography of 100 pages in four months. It took five months, and the finished manuscript was 101 pages—not counting the photographs.

And so the winter of '95 was one of recovery (April counts as a winter month in Vermont). I would see the physical therapist first thing in the morning; she would "manipulate" my shoulder and prescribe the stretching exercises and the weight lifting that she wanted me to do in the afternoon. I would write my memoir in the middle of the day; in the late afternoon or early evening I would go to my wrestling room and follow the orders of the physical therapist.

To explain "my" wrestling room—it is about 25 feet from my office in the Vermont house. (Between the office and the wrestling room is a small locker room: a toilet, three sinks, two showers, a sauna.) My wrestling mat is equivalent to the in-bounds area of a regulation mat. About a dozen jump ropes, of varying lengths, hang from pegs at one end of the room; at the other end is an area for weight lifting—a couple of weight benches and two racks of free weights. There's also a stationary bike and a treadmill, and lots of shelves for knee pads, elbow pads, head gear, spools of tape—and about a dozen pairs of wrestling shoes, in a somewhat limited range of sizes. (Brendan's feet are only a little bigger than mine; Colin's are only a little bigger than Brendan's.)

There are over 300 photographs on the walls; there aren't many of me, and even fewer of Everett—and not a lot of room remaining for the photos of Everett, which I presume will come. Most of the pictures are of Colin and Brendan, together with the bracket sheets from the tournaments they won. There are twelve medals, five trophies, and one plaque; only the plaque is mine. I never won any medals or trophies, because I never won a wrestling tournament.

I didn't really "win" the plaque. In 1992, I was selected as one of the first 10 members in the Hall of Outstanding Americans by the National Wrestling Hall of Fame in Stillwater, Oklahoma. These "Outstanding Americans" were not necessarily outstanding wrestlers, although a few of them were; we were all chosen for being outstanding at something else, and for having also (in our fashion) wrestled.

I am honored to be a member of the National Wrestling Hall of Fame, although I'm embarrassed to have gained entry through the back door—meaning for my other accomplishments, *not* my wrestling or my coaching. I feel privileged to have been in the same wrestling room with some of the wrestling and coaching members of the Hall of Fame—George Martin, Dave McCuskey, Rex Peery, Dan Gable.

You may be surprised to learn of a couple of other "Outstanding Americans" whom the National Wrestling Hall of Fame has honored: Kirk Douglas and General H. Norman Schwarzkopf. I'm surprised that, as of this writing, my fellow novelist Ken Kesey *hasn't* been selected as a member; Mr. Kesey's wrestling credentials are a whole lot better than mine. He is still ranked as one of the top 10 wrestlers (most career wins) at the University of Oregon, where he graduated in '57. And in '82, at the age of 47, Kesey won the AAU Masters Championships at 198 pounds.

I suspect that after the Senate confirms General Charles C. ("Brute") Krulak's promotion to four-star rank, and General Krulak is officially serving on the Joint Chiefs of Staff, the new Commandant of the Marines will also become a member in the Hall of Outstanding Americans at Stillwater. Described by *The New York Times* as "a diminutive dynamo of a man"—he was a 121-pounder at Exeter and a 123-pounder at Navy—Chuck was a platoon leader and company commander during two tours of duty in the Vietnam War, and later served as commander of the counterguerrilla-warfare school in Okinawa. Thereafter, General Krulak was commanding general of the Marine Corps Combat Development Command in Quantico, Virginia, and—just prior to President Clinton's nominating him as the next Commandant of the Marines—Krulak commanded 82,000 marines and 600 combat aircraft in the Pacific. (In the event of war in Korea or the Persian Gulf, General Krulak would have commanded all the marines there.) But as a member of the National Wrestling Hall of Fame, which I assume he will be, Chuck Krulak will probably feel as I do: namely, that the honor is undeserved.

Thus my plaque from the National Wrestling Hall of Fame occupies the far corner of a shelf in my wrestling room, where it stands a little sheepishly, looking unearned beside the hardware and the ribbons that Colin and Brendan won outright. I go to such lengths to describe the territory of my wrestling room and its proximity to my office because I want you to understand that the distance between my writing and my wrestling is never great; indeed, in the winter I was writing "The Imaginary Girlfriend," the distance was only 25 feet.

For four months, I didn't venture farther than that 25-foot path—with two exceptions. The first was a trip to Aspen in the middle of March. I spent less than a week with Colin and Brendan in Colorado. I couldn't ski; I went to the gym and repeated the rehabilitation exercises that my physical therapist in Vermont had given me, and I paddled around in the heated pool and the hot tub with Everett. I had some very pleasant dinners with the Salters, Kay and Jim, and then it was back to Vermont to finish the "Girlfriend"—only I couldn't finish it; not before leaving for France in April, for the French translation of *A Son of the Circus*.

After most of my interviews in Paris, in the lobby of the Hotel Lutétia, a photographer would drag me to a small plot of greenery (less than a park) off the boulevard Raspail and attempt to position me beside a statue of the French novelist François Mauriac. I refused to be photographed beside the statue of Mauriac, largely because the statue is 15 feet tall—you may recall that I'm only five feet eight—but also because I thought that Mauriac looked extremely undernourished and depressed. Possibly he was mortified to be photographed alongside every visiting author who was staying at the Lutétia.

That was Paris: I was brooding about not having finished "The Imaginary Girlfriend" before I had to leave for France, and I was constantly and unsubtly being compared to Mauriac. One of his critics once said that God surely disapproved of what Mauriac had written, to which Mauriac admirably responded: "God doesn't care at all—what we write—but when we do it right, He can use it." (I kept telling one photographer after another that God couldn't possibly find a use for a photograph of John Irving with François Mauriac, but the photographers were uncomprehending; one of them misinterpreted my refusal to be photographed with Mauriac as a sure sign of religious zealotry.)

Back in Vermont, April dragged on—so did the "Girlfriend." In May I spent less than a week with Colin and Brendan in California. By then, my rehabilitation exercises were only two hours a day, and I discovered that I could once again carry Everett on my shoulders; we took him to Disneyland, where, admittedly, Colin and Brendan carried him around more often and more easily than I did. On the plane back East from L.A., I was still revising "The Imaginary Girlfriend," which I wouldn't finish before June.

An intractable phenomenon of writing an autobiography is that you begin to miss the people you are writing about; I don't ever miss the characters in my novels, although some of my readers have told me that *they* miss them. I found myself wanting to call up people I hadn't seen or spoken to in more than 30 years. In most cases, the motivation was more than nostalgia; I couldn't remember all the details—what was so-and-so's weight class, and did he win a Big 10 title, or did he even *place*?

I called Kay Gallagher, Cliff's widow, a couple of times. Cliff had done so many things I couldn't keep them all straight. It was nice to talk to Kay, but it made me miss Cliff.

As for coincidence, the novelist's companion, Don Hendrie's death (in March) coincided precisely with that point in my autobiography where Hendrie was to make his first appearance. My friend Phillip Borsos also died last winter; he was the movie director who made *The Grey Fox*, and with whom I'd been trying to make the film of *The Cider House Rules*—for almost 10 years. Phillip was only 41; his death (cancer), in addition to its own sadness, called back to mind the death of Tony Richardson. (Tony directed *The Hotel New Hampshire*—he died of AIDS in 1991. My friend George Roy Hill, now debilitated with Parkinson's, directed *The World According to Garp*.) Tony used to call me rather late at night and ask me if I'd read anything good lately; he was a voracious reader. Thinking of Tony often puts me in a mood to call people, too. As I was coming to the end of "The Imaginary Girlfriend," I was calling people left and right.

On Memorial Day weekend, I called my old friend Eric Ross in Crested Butte. While I'd been in France, avoiding the Mauriac photo opportunities, Eric had been golfing in Ireland with a bad case of gout. I have never golfed, nor had gout, but the combination struck me as a cruel and comedic affliction.

Thus inspired, I decided to call Vincent Buonomano. I speculated, stupidly, that after Buonomano had graduated from Mount Pleasant High School, he'd never left the Providence area. I called information in Rhode Island and was informed that there was only one Vincent Buonomano in the environs of Providence; actually, he lived in Warwick. I made the call.

A girl answered; she sounded like a teenager. I asked for Vincent Buonomano. The girl said, "Who's calling?"

"He probably doesn't remember me," I said. "I haven't seen him since he was in high school."

She went off screaming for him. "Dad!" Or maybe she said, "Daddy!" I had the impression of a large house and a large family.

Mr. Buonomano was very friendly to me on the phone, but he wasn't the same Vincent Buonomano who'd pinned me in the pit— with less than a minute remaining in the third period. The nice man on the phone said that he occasionally got calls for the other Buonomano, the wrestler, and once some bills for "the wrestler" had been sent to the wrong Buonomano's address. The Mr. Buonomano who talked to me told me that he thought the Buonomano

I was looking for had gone to college and was now a physician—
because one of the bills was seeking repayment of a student loan,
and because one of the bills was addressed to a Dr. Vincent Buonomano. (I speculated that he specialized in necks.) But I couldn't
find him. He had slipped away, surely never remembering me.

It made me so sad I simply had to call Anthony Pieranunzi.
There was a greater likelihood that Pieranunzi would remember
me, I thought: our matches had been close. But the operator told
me that there was no Anthony Pieranunzi in East Providence, and
only one in Providence; it had to be him, I was certain—I called
immediately. An extremely likable woman answered the phone.
I instantly remembered Pieranunzi's girlfriend. (It's possible she
was his sister—she was a knockout, anyway.) I imagined I was
talking to the high-school sweetheart of my archrival—now a
devoted wife of some 30-plus years.

I said something truly stupid, like: "Is this the home of
Anthony Pieranunzi, the wrestler?"

The woman laughed. "Lord, no," she said. She'd heard of the
wrestler; there had been other phone calls—and, of course, bills
sent to the wrong address. (Bills had become a common theme—
they were perpetually being sent to the wrong address.) The
woman told me that someone had once called her husband and
asked him if he was *the* Anthony Pieranunzi. It was *the* Anthony
Pieranunzi I was looking for, of course. But he had slipped away
with Vincent Buonomano, neither of them ever knowing how
important they were to me.

I felt like talking to a friend.

Following a conversation with Sonny Greenhalgh, which deteriorated into a dispute concerning whether John Carr had wrestled at 147 pounds or at 157, I decided to call John Carr. The conversation with Sonny, as with most conversations with Sonny, entailed a fair amount of Sherman Moyer. To this day, it stands as an outrage in Sonny's life that he lost twice, in the same season, to Moyer—although this was 33 years ago. (Sonny was an All-American; Moyer wasn't. I'm guessing that this is what makes the losses unacceptable to Sonny.) To this day, my sympathy for Sonny is moderated by the fact that, at the time, I was cheering for Moyer, who was my teammate; I didn't know Sonny then, except that I knew he was a highly regarded 130-pounder at Syracuse. My sympathy for Sonny's two losses to Moyer is also lessened by the fact that I wrestled Moyer every day for an entire wrestling season; as such, I lost to him every day—a mere *two* defeats at the hands of Moyer seems like no disgrace and no special hardship to *me*. Sonny and I *always* talk about this, notwithstanding the fact that we have other things in common to talk about. (I coached Sonny Greenhalgh's son, Jon, when Jon was a teammate of Brendan's at Vermont Academy; Jon Greenhalgh won a New England title in 1989.)

But this time my conversation with Sonny concerned John Carr—was he a 147-pounder or a 157-pounder? What turned the talk to Carr was that Sonny had heard that Carr's dad had died, and I remembered Mr. Carr fondly—from the time he'd enthusiastically stepped in and coached me at West Point. By the time I got off the phone with Sonny, there was another thing I wanted to talk to John Carr about: I knew he'd won a New England title the year before we both went to Pittsburgh, but I couldn't remember if he'd been a PG at Andover or at Cheshire—in both cases, in my memory, the uniforms were blue.

At the New England tournament that year, the Outstanding Wrestler award was given to Anthony Pieranunzi, the presently elusive East Providence standout, who'd kept me from winning a New England title; John Carr arguably deserved the award. Pieranunzi was good, but the talk in the locker room suggested that Carr was better; I don't really know, because I never wrestled Carr. And that was why I believed Carr had wrestled at 157 pounds: if he'd wrestled at 147, I *would* have wrestled him—he would have been a workout partner, at least a few times. (As a 130-pounder, I used to work out with the 147-pounders occasionally, but the 157-pounders were too big.)

When I called information, the operator informed me that there were seven guys named John Carr in the Wilkes-Barre area of Pennsylvania, but it didn't take long to track him down. I talked to the wife of the wrong John Carr, and to four or five other wrong John Carrs, too; they *all* said, "Oh, you want the wrestler." Or: "You want the coach."

By the time I got him, it was all over town that I was looking for him; he was expecting my call. Carr remembered me, but not my face; he couldn't put me with a face, he said. I'm not surprised; in fact, I was surprised he remembered me at all—as I said, we never wrestled each other and my wrestling was hardly anything worth *watching*. If John Carr had had a minute to watch the other wrestlers in the Pitt wrestling room, there were a lot of better guys to watch than me.

I was right: Carr had been a 157-pounder, and he told me he'd been a PG at Cheshire when he won the New England's—*not* at Andover. I told him I was sorry to hear about his dad. Carr wasn't coaching anymore; he complained that the influence of freestyle (international) wrestling had hurt high-school and collegiate (or folkstyle) wrestling. For one thing, there was not enough pinning—wrestling wasn't as aggressive as it used to be, John Carr said. I share his view. I was never a fan of freestyle. As I once heard Dan Gable say of collegiate wrestling: "If you can't get off the bottom, you can't win." (In freestyle, you don't have to be able to get off the bottom; the referee blows his whistle and *lets* you off the bottom—you can spend almost the whole match in the neutral position, on your feet. And so I knew what John Carr was thinking: he was thinking, How tough is *that?* In a freestyle match, I *might* have been able to beat Sherman Moyer; it was when I was on the bottom that Moyer killed me.)

Carr told me that Mike Johnson was still coaching at Du Bois, and that Warnick's kid—or one of Warnick's kids—had been pretty successful on the mat at West Point. I remembered seeing the name Warnick in the Army lineup and wondering if this was a child of the Warnick who'd arm-dragged me to death in my one winter at Pittsburgh. After John Carr and I said goodnight, and I hung up the phone, I realized that I'd not asked him if Warnick's kid had learned his father's killer arm-drag. I almost called Carr back. But when I start the phone calls, especially at night, I have to stop somewhere. If I keep going, I get in a mood to call *everybody*.

Of course I'd like to call Cliff Gallagher—if only to hear him say, "Not even a zebra, Johnny." And I often think about calling Ted Seabrooke, before I remember that I can't. Ted wasn't a big talker—not compared to Cliff—but Ted was insightful at interrupting me, and at contradicting me, too. I'd be saying something and he'd say, "That sounds pretty stupid to me." Or: "Why would you want to do that?" And: "Do what you know how to do." Or: "What's worked for you before?" Cliff used to say that Ted could clear the air.

It still seems unacceptable that both Ted and Cliff are dead, although Cliff (given normal life expectancy) would almost surely be dead by now—Cliff was born in 1897, which would make him all of 98, if he were alive today. I think it broke Cliff's heart that Ted died first—Ted died young. And Ted fooled us: after the diabetes, which he got control of, he had some healthy years; then the cancer came and killed him in the fall of 1980. He was 59.

For Coach Seabrooke's memorial service in Phillips Church, there were more wrestlers than I ever saw in the Exeter wrestling room. Bobby Thompson, one of Exeter's ex-heavyweights—and arguably the biggest-ever New England Class A Champion in the Unlimited class—sang "Amazing Grace." (Bobby is the school minister at Exeter today.)

It was an outrage to all his wrestlers that Ted was dead. He'd seemed indomitable to us. He had twice been struck by lightning, while playing golf; both times he'd survived. Both times he'd said, "It's just one of those things."

After Ted's memorial service, I remember Cliff Gallagher grabbing me with a Russian arm-tie and whispering in my ear: "It should have been me, Johnny—it should have been me." My arm was sore for days. Cliff had a nasty Russian arm-tie. At the time, Cliff was 83.

I don't lead a hectic life. It's not every night, or every week—or even every month—that I feel the need to "clear the air." Most nights, I don't even look at the telephone. Other times, the unringing phone seems to summon all the unreachable people in the past. I think of that poem of Rilke's, about the corpse: *"Und einer ohne Namen/lag bar und reinlich da und gab Gesetze"* ("And one without a name/lay clean and naked there, and gave commands"). That is the telephone on certain nights: it is the unreachable past— the dead demanding to give us advice. On those nights, I'm sorry I can't talk to Ted.